THE ROLE OF THE SELF
IN CONFLICTS AND STRUGGLE

BOOKS BY
EDWARD LeROY LONG, JR.
Published by The Westminster Press

THE ROLE OF THE SELF IN CONFLICTS AND STRUGGLE

CONSCIENCE AND COMPROMISE: *An Outline of Protestant Casuistry*

RELIGIOUS BELIEFS OF AMERICAN SCIENTISTS

THE CHRISTIAN RESPONSE TO THE ATOMIC CRISIS

THE
ROLE OF THE SELF
IN CONFLICTS
AND STRUGGLE

by

Edward LeRoy Long, Jr.

THE WESTMINSTER PRESS
Philadelphia

LIBRARY OF CONGRESS CATALOG CARD NO. 62–18067

PRINTED IN THE UNITED STATES OF AMERICA

CONTENTS

PREFACE

THIS discussion is written in the attempt to describe the kinds of personal and social attitudes that are fruitful in the transformation of struggle from crass and blatant partisanship into informed and sensitive stewardship over the vitalities and instrumentalities of human life. It is primarily concerned with the way in which Christians should espouse whatever causes they see fit to serve rather than to suggest the specific positions Christians ought to embrace. It admits by silence on certain policy matters that Christians come to different decisions about some questions in our day, but suggests their obligation to support the cause of their loyalty with personal maturity and spiritual sensitivity. This approach has been adopted to bear witness to an aspect of the truth sometimes overlooked, and not to imply that men can ignore issues that surely must be faced in other contexts.

Much theological discussion of conflict during recent years has been preoccupied with the moral implications of war and peace. The question of Christian participation in armed conflict has been argued from both pacifist and nonpacifist positions. More recent discussions have cast the problem in terms of a difference between a just war and a moral crusade. It is hoped that this book has something to say relevant to the more recent discussions of the issue.

But it is no longer sufficient, if once it was a primary question, to consider Christian obligation either to par-

7

ticipate or to refuse to participate in coercive struggle.
The particular problem of military conflict is but one
facet of a more general human situation in which conflict
occurs in several forms and on many levels. The political
order and the scientific endeavor to subdue nature for
human betterment also contain struggle. Any theological
perspective in touch with man's total cultural life will
analyze the kinds of subtle and covert tensions born of
man's effort to subjugate nature for human benefit as well
as the obvious kinds of conflict associated with political
life. It will look at the actual kinds of loyalties and attitudes expressed by men in the several forms of struggle.

This book falls naturally into three divisions. The first
three chapters are concerned with definitions of terms
basic to the entire argument. The second three chapters
set forth certain crucial problems that arise from the
presence of struggle in human life. The final chapters explore the Christian contribution toward spiritual maturity
in facing the problems inherent in human conflict. The
several forms of human struggle are analyzed together and
their common features made the focus of attention. Further elaboration of the purpose and structure of the book
is found in the argument itself.

Despite the help of gracious friends, the preparation of
a book is no exception to the rule that struggle is a characteristic dimension of all human existence. Even while
writing about man's struggle with nature, the grass must
be mowed. At the same time one is thinking about political responsibility the obligations of citizenship in college
and community must be fulfilled. It is sometimes easier to
write about struggle detached from the reality than when
one is involved in it, but undoubtedly less real. The draft-
ing of this volume was done in respites between much
activity. It is sent off with the hope that, despite its limitations, it may speak relevantly in times of turmoil.

E.L.L., JR.

Oberlin, Ohio

I

CONQUEST, COMPETITION, AND COERCION: THE FORMS OF STRUGGLE

STRUGGLE is one of the most characteristic features of human life. We live in a world in which life is preserved only by effort, where ruthlessness frequently obtains the spoils, and where men rule by the manipulation of power. Men fight germs and hold back the ravages of storms, the skilled surpass the simple, and the strong exercise dominion over the weak. Struggle occurs on all levels of human life and in many forms. Some struggle involves men in the effort to subdue the world of nature; other struggle involves friendly, and at times less than friendly, rivalry between parties seeking to outdo each other in the attainment of certain goals; still other struggle involves the effort to destroy an opponent or overcome an antagonist.

The place of struggle in human life has been both decried and glorified, yet in both reactions its presence has been acknowledged. Efforts to reject the place of struggle in human life stand in telling juxtaposition to efforts to glorify it as the high good of man. Religions like Taoism tend to reject struggle, while others, like Shintoism, tend to glorify it. Few are oblivious to its presence. In the thought of some interpreters struggle is the symbol of the human plight and understood as a prime obstacle to self-fulfillment, while in the evaluations of others struggle is

9

the channel by which men express their pledged devotion to that which they hold most dear. Struggle persists even in those cultures dominated by a religious quietism, and peace is a goal even in religions that teach men to strive in defense of the truth in which they believe.

Not only is struggle widespread in human life but it may grip men in a vise of circumstance that seems to defy their mastery over it. It was not an existentialist writer but a man of public affairs who penned these words:

> Human existence has always been a race with catastrophe, but never has the race been so close, or the threatening catastrophe so universal and so overwhelming. It seems like a drama played in a dream—a drama in which all mankind constitutes both the actors and the spectators. We watch ourselves on the stage in the grip of evil forces which we seem powerless to resist—fear, hate, face-saving pride, misunderstanding, intolerance, ineptitude, and moral inadequacy. We know that a war fought with our new weapons will turn the world into a gigantic slaughterhouse and bury the hopes and monuments of our race beyond recovery. But the play goes on to its apparently inevitable denouement, and frozen to our seats, we do not know how to stop it. (Raymond B. Fosdick, "Christmas Thoughts in 'A World Gone Mad,'" in *The New York Times Magazine*, December 22, 1957, p. 5.)

It may not be within our power to decide whether or not to be involved in the realities of struggle, though we may to some extent determine the quality of our reaction to it. But even this control is tempered by the ways in which struggle exerts far-reaching effects upon the characters and attitudes of men who engage in it. Struggle can bring forth the heroic best and the demonic worst from men. It can lead to satisfaction and produce bitter jealousy. It can prompt sacrifice and devotion as well as turn loose passions of hatred and vindictive anger. Struggle produces calluses on the hands of the farmer, ulcers in the stomach of the businessman, medals on the chest of the soldier. As an outgrowth of deep loyalties it becomes charged with feeling and emotion, and never more so than when related to religion and patriotism.

The moral and spiritual problems created by struggle seem more intense than the moral and spiritual problems produced by other aspects of human life. In dramatic writing from that of the ancient tragedians to that of modern poets and playwrights struggle has furnished a pregnant source of plots with which to portray the human being in both his grandeur and his misery. Struggle deeply affects the selfhood of those who are involved—by choice or accident—in the rigors, uncertainties, and heartbreak as well as the victories, achievements, and joy that attend its movements and mark its outcomes. Struggle shapes the loyalties and determines the spiritual conditions of all it touches. To know what a man strives for in life is to know much of his frame of mind and bent of will. When it is said that someone "wholeheartedly" engages in struggle the very choice of phrase bears witness to the reality involved. A man's heart—his self—his total being—becomes deeply and intimately involved in struggle, and is frequently changed and altered by it. It is because struggle relates to the selfhood of man and involves questions of his loyalties that it is related to religious concerns and begs for analysis with the tools of theological reflection.

Our first task, however, is to delineate the forms of struggle. In the discussion that follows we explore three kinds of human conflict. The first relates to man's conquest of space and his subjugation of nature; the second relates to man's competition with other men in the scramble for prestige and status; the third relates to the coercive conflicts represented by war and social turmoil. Close scrutiny of these divisions will show that we are likely to be involved in a study of semantics as well as a description of reality, for words used to describe struggle sometimes have double meanings. When we use the term "conquest," for example, we may mean either the struggle of man against nature or the coerced victory of one man over another. But we are permitted to define our terms, and we choose to use the term "conquest" for man's struggle to subdue the primal forces of the universe for his benefit and "coercion" to denote the struggle against opponents who would deny men the rights of life, liberty, and the pursuit of happiness.

By using the term "conquest" for man's struggle with nature we can underscore a conviction that the fruits of knowledge and technology do not come cheaply. We have ticker-tape parades to honor men who conquer space as well as for those who win in war. A transatlantic flyer in one era and astronauts in another ride the same strewn path of honor as returning generals. Moreover, they undergo the same threats to life and limb and suffer the same privations of personal convenience. It is possible to overplay the difficulties that are entailed in conquering nature and remaining master of it, but the modern optimist has tended to underplay them. The erstwhile hope that improved technology would free men from the dimensions of struggle is a dream that could be cherished only in a time when the firstfruits of technical progress overshadowed its genuine cost.

Whoever has hoed weeds during a rainy season or watered plants during a dry one appreciates full well the phrase from Genesis about "the sweat of the face," but the city dweller knows the same reality and describes it as "the daily grind." There is a strange irony in the life of the suburbanite who escapes the treadmill at the office by hoeing weeds in a garden and fighting crabgrass in a lawn. The very activities that to the farmer are humdrum at best and burdensome at worst are to the suburbanite a source of escape and perhaps even of joy. Does this mean that the struggle of daily work becomes a burden only when we are chained to it by sheer necessity or forced to it by the need to support ourselves and loved ones? Or do we become unhappy because the freedom of the self can soar with vision beyond the grim necessity, and, unlike the animals, can ask why things are not easier in God's creation?

It would be utter foolishness to deny the conquests of drudgery and degrading routines that have occurred through the application of technology for the benefit of man. There are few people who would return to the farmhouse of the nineteenth century with its wood stove and outside water pump. But despite the great advances in standards of living, our lives today are no less marked by the reality of struggle—albeit in differing, and even more difficult, forms. The "sweat of the face" is still here, in figurative terms at least. The tensions, anxieties, and demands of maintaining life are no less real in a plush and prosperous America than in the days of our forefathers or in the primitive conditions of less developed areas of the world. Indeed, if the literature of our time is any guide to our innermost feelings, the tensions are the more oppressive precisely because they are more advanced, and the beatniks who yearn for "no sweat" may indicate that for some at least the pressure has become too great.

If the sweatshop and mop bucket are the symbols of an age now past for millions in our day, the assembly line and overly crowded appointment calendar are the symbols of the present time. Those inclined to yearn for the former are entitled to romantic nostalgia, but it ought not to be an escape from the task at hand. We have been set into the midst of a life which, despite the form we give to it, faces us with struggle and demands of us perseverance and effort. The "sweat of the face" is with us to stay; to yearn for its evaporation is to wish for the impossible.

But if the struggle represented by daily drudgery eats and gnaws at men's zeal and wears down their high resolves and good resolutions, the struggle involved in the conquest of space and time impels men to outbursts of enthusiasm and feats of endurance. Men seem inwardly impelled to conquer the unknown and to bring the far domains of the universe under their control. They will undergo privation, expend enormous energy, suffer discomfort and fatigue, cast aside all other values—including the surety of life itself—to attain this goal. Men are driven by the irresistible urge to conquer, not only the frontiers of geography and the regions of space, but the very secrets of nature herself.

Conquest of this type is more frequently considered an adventure than it is deemed a kind of struggle—but the semantics make little difference in a space capsule. In an age dominated by scientific curiosity and technological achievement we tend to glory in the effort to conquer and subdue the environment of man. But the process is hard work. It demands patience, endurance, and fortitude. Even the air-conditioned scientific research laboratory may demand of its occupants a kind of self-sacrifice and personal denial not appreciated by outsiders. For every rocket that sails into space there are many that blow to bits and fall to earth, destroying not only themselves but the enthusiasm and hopes of their creators and dashing to the ground not only the instruments they carry but the expectations pinned upon them. It is surely right to call the attempted conquest of nature a form of struggle and to recognize its affinities to other experiences in which men must do battle for what they get.

A second form of struggle is competition. This involves friendly, and frequently less than friendly, rivalry between individuals or groups of men. It is found in both hidden and in open forms, and has been both praised and damned by participants and observers alike. If men are driven by the urge to conquer, they are perhaps driven even more by the urge to win. The urge to win spurs men to noble sacrifice and tempts them to ignoble means, goads them to ingenuity and tempts them to treachery. When the urge to win is kept within the bounds of communal standards, competition results; if the bounds are broken, another form of struggle takes over.

The most zestful type of competition is the game. It is a form of competition in which the striving parties are carefully matched, the rules of procedure explicitly stated, and the outcome gracefully accepted after it has been determined by the rules. The game is a form of struggle— but it is a highly sublimated type of struggle kept healthy by not only a common acknowledgment of rules but by an ordered provision for their enforcement. The umpire or referee symbolizes in his position the acceptance of a common standard to which both participants give higher loyalty than to themselves, and he sees to it that in the pressure of events the covenantal basis of the game prevails. Good sportsmanship is a high spiritual achievement made possible by careful attention to the conditions within which it is to operate.

The political competition of the party system within mature societies depends upon much the same conditions. The "umpire" in the case of politics is a more elaborate system of checks and balances, but without the covenant of agreement that binds each side to acceptance of the outcome and the rules for determining it, stable political order is an impossibility. When corruption exceeds certain limits or the acceptance of the process falls below certain standards the stability of representative government is undercut. There is no competition in tyranny because one side overwhelms all others; in anarchy the conflict of vitalities becomes so great that no commonly acknowledged set of procedures is possible.

Games can be corroded by the acids of jealousy, and politics can degenerate into struggles of power and intrigue. We may apply the term "competition" to struggles only as long as there is a standard or authority to which all the participants will repair, even if only under pressure. The school that has turned its stadium into an instrument of prestige may stop at few lengths to secure the victory upon which such prestige depends, but it is not likely to ignore the mandates of the athletic conference to which it belongs. It may pursue the game with ruthless vigor, eclipsing the zest that goes with playing for sport, but even so it won't murder the referee or let a frenzied crowd make good a threat to do so. The political party may buy votes, stuff the ballot boxes, and engage in all sorts of techniques to win an election, but it will not overthrow the electoral system itself by force and violence.

But the game is not the only form that competition takes, and there are rivalries in human life that are not sublimated with the instruments of mature and stable political orders. Much competition stems from personal and social thrusts for prestige, and emerges as much from a mood and spirit as from a particular lineup of contenders. The forms and techniques of such competition defy easy description or neat cataloging by type. They are as varied as the clashes between individuals or between groups are numerous, and may even set an individual in conflict with the group. Fisticuffs between young boys; jealousy spats between adolescent girls; efforts to impress one's peers with prowess or possessions; jockeying for power within a social club or business enterprise—the list is endless and the forms as novel and ingenious as the mind of man. Competition begins early and lasts late and affects even those societies that would disavow it. It may find expression in the realm of nature: trees too closely planted in a forest are worth careful study; the pecking order of the henhouse is proverbial.

One form of competitive struggle springs from pride of possessions. The young owner of a shiny new bicycle is no less apt to be affected by this attitude than is the venerable owner of large wealth. Indeed, pride of possession can be insidious when the visibility of the possession is high even though its intrinsic worth is not great. Thus pride of possession may be even stronger in middle-class suburbia than in the estates of country club acres. After all, a person can use just so much house. Conspicuous consumption has an optimum expressibility beyond which it is subject to a law of diminishing returns.

The subtle and covert competition involving property symbols is backed by gnawing urges. When young Johnny says to Stephen, "See my shiny new bike," Stephen is apt to sneer, "But where's its horn?" If the new bike is paraded as a means of showing status, no less can the counterthrust be a means of maintaining it. A new bike is no threat to the owner of an old bike if its fresh appearance can be cancelled by a criticism of its adequacy. Every possession has limitations, and can be discredited by those who would fend off the status claims of its owner. The new bike holds the obvious edge over the old bike only in the mind of its owner, and even if he obtains a horn to round out its complement of equipment, the owner of the older bike can claim that his vehicle is better "broken in." Unless possessions are exactly equal, which they seldom are even in an age of mass production, the mere possession of an item is a dubious road to status. Those who travel such a road will frequently discover that each new turn only leads across a barren waste to another turn, and that each newly acquired possession invites further kinds of comparisons between the self and other owners.

But men compare themselves, not only in terms of their possessions, but in terms of their membership within exclusive groups. The literature of contemporary sociology and the observations of popular commentaries document this trait in wide scope and explicit detail. This is no new thing: that status function of clan and tribe is as real in primitive and ancient cultures as the status function of the club is in ours. What may be new is the diversity of such clubs, and the need to belong to several of them in order to achieve the kind of overall acceptance that a primitive might experience within his tribe alone.

If membership within a special group carried with it the satisfactions of status, life might be made reasonably tolerable by joining it, but the average group is itself a stage of competitive struggle for status within the organization. Because such struggle is more intimate, it is frequently more bitter and the rivalries of in-group strife are even more devastating than are those outside the organization. A person can surely win a national cereal-box contest against competitors in other states with less tension than arises when he defeats a close friend in the lodge election. To make experience more intimate and more personal is not necessarily to make it more tolerable.

Some of the fast-run races of our day bring together conquest and competition. Through conquest man seeks, not only to subdue nature and bring the resources of the world to useful purpose, but to beat other men at doing so. He seeks to enhance his status in contrast to his fellowmen —to be the first to climb Mount Everest, to sail under the polar ice, to place a satellite around the moon. Competition may actually prompt and hasten conquest. How much would the nations of the world spend on space research if other nations were not competing to be first in visiting the outer regions?

In competitive struggle men engage in contests of skill and power conducted under rules to which all conflicting parties give assent—if only in minimal terms. In another type of struggle one party undertakes to coerce others to the acceptance of the rules themselves or to submission without regard for rules. In coercive struggle victory must be obtained by using power, prestige, or position to enforce the will of the winner upon the loser. If not the most prevalent, coercion is usually the most bitter and trouble-some kind of struggle. Instead of contest, such struggle involves fighting; instead of games, battles; instead of rivalry, hostility and hatred.

There is some coercion in human life that involves no overt sign of struggle, either because the weak submit passively to the strong when the power balance is radically unequal or because men submit to the will of the ruler when the authority of the party exercising coercion is acknowledged. A police state exercises coercion but does not necessarily use violence, even though the iron heel of the tyrant never rests securely on its victims. A parent may use mild and sober coercion in bringing up the child, without being caught in a knock-down battle. Coercion springs from the use and possession of power, and power rests in turn upon the possibility of inflicting privation upon or granting rewards to another person. Latent power may be tacitly acknowledged by a weak man in the face of a stronger antagonist, in which case there is coercion without resistance, victory without violence. To condone the latent exercise of power because outwardly things are calm is a mistake of judgment; to condemn it without scrutiny of circumstance may involve no less an error. Both tyranny and authority rest upon the latent power of coercion, and while there may be no legitimate tyrannies, there are legitimate authorities.

War is the obvious instance of violent coercive struggle. War involves the deliberate effort to force others to sub-mit to the will of a protagonist or be destroyed. War is frequently fought in defense of a cherished value or for the extension of the power of a group. Today, at least, it knows few rules and is marked by the effort totally to destroy an opponent. The ability to inflict privation or pain is mobilized in modern war to a scale undreamed of even three decades ago. From the human perspective, death is the ultimate privation, and when it can be inflicted wholesale the moral consequences are as grave as the power realities are stark.

At one time war was more nearly like competition than it is today. People took it seriously, to be sure, but there were rules for the "game," and all civilized peoples acknowledged them. Chivalry was a virtue based upon a code of honor and requiring knights to fight like men rather than to stab each other behind their backs or murder whole populations by remote control. Today war depends upon surprise and intrigue, and the army that lets its scruples get in the way is likely to lose the battle. During the Middle Ages, armies laid down their weapons for the weekend observance of the Sabbath, a practice long since abandoned even by pious men. In the First World War there was a commonly accepted set of rules for the treatment of war prisoners, but in Korea an enemy not destroyed on the battlefield became fair game as a prisoner.

Violent coercion is also evident in the kind of mob action sporadically experienced in segregated cities that are under court orders to desegregate their public facilities. Such action is as threatening as it is unpleasant, intended to be as coercive as it is hysterical. It can find itself taking furious vengeance upon all who, standing in its way, become identified as scapegoats for its anger. Narrower in its scope yet less disciplined in its procedures than war, mob hysteria is no easy thing to control even where there is a will to do so. It has coercive impact because it can threaten privation of liberty and the infliction of pain.

But coercive struggle can take nonviolent forms as well as bloody ones, and many voices in our day would extol certain types of nonviolent coercion as morally superior and pragmatically more feasible than armed conflict. The plausibility of these claims is heightened by the relatively high degree of success enjoyed so far in the use of nonviolent coercion, but the limited scope of these applications may leave the final determination in doubt. We do not yet have enough evidence about nonviolent coercion to know very much about its effectiveness. In employing a salt march against the British, Gandhi captured the imaginations of many persons looking for an alternative to violent forms of coercion, but he has likewise prompted the sneers of those who claim that his victories were less a demonstration of his power than a consequence of the goodwill and humanitarian temper of the English rulers. In seeking to break bus and lunch-counter segregation, the leaders of the boycott and sit-in demonstrations in the Southern states have won the admiration of many observers. One of their chief spokesmen, Martin Luther King, has emerged as a leader of enormous stature and a writer of persuasive power. Whether the techniques of nonviolence are useful in other areas of social conflict remains in doubt, and to endorse them as cure-alls is as dangerous as to discount their value is stupid.

Nonviolent coercion depends for its final sanction upon the capacity of a group to ignore or discount the usual sanctions of coercion. Instead of fearing privation, it accepts it; instead of protecting the self against pain, it accepts without rancor or retaliation the injuries and insults that come as a consequence of its stand. That the behavior required to conduct oneself in a manner suitable to accomplish such ends must be carefully cultivated and specially nursed goes without saying, and the evidence would seem to suggest that groups long accustomed to privation and submerged conditions can learn the art more readily than social classes that have been used to temporal lordship. We have not yet experienced a conflict in which two sides committed to the techniques of nonviolence and skilled in using them have struggled against each other. Such pragmatic advantages as nonviolent means of struggle seem to possess may stem more from their capacity to neutralize the normal sanctions of coercive violence than from their inherent power as a procedural device. We do not know what might happen in a case in which nonviolence becomes pitted against nonviolence.

Some would argue that such conflict cannot take place because the very spiritual qualities needed to use "soul force" would insure the possibility of amicable settlements between two parties dedicated to its use. It is frequently assumed, perhaps because nonviolent coercion has been employed to date largely by groups fighting for transparently justifiable ends, that only people dedicated to the achievement of righteousness can muster the kind of resolution and courage needed to conduct their struggle by such means. But who knows? What guarantees the identity of nonviolence and virtue? Deviltry is not incapable of beguilement, and Nietzsche's superman was to rule without bloodshed. Paul Ramsey has questioned the identification of Christian action *as such* by the criterion of its nonviolent nature:

Concerning nonviolent resistance, like any other act of resistance, the Christian must ask whether any such thing is permitted and required by Christian love. And as with any other tactical action appearing in the public sphere, its justice and its lawfulness must be subjected to inquiry by the Christian and the responsible citizen. (*Christian Ethics and the Sit-in*, p. xiv. Association Press, 1961. Used by permission.)

To regard a certain kind of pressure as morally superior merely because it is exercised without recourse to violence is to narrow the basis of judgment too severely. It is to measure legitimacy in terms only of means, and leaves aside the question of motive and end. The exponents of nonviolent coercion have long spoken fully about the importance of motives as well as means, and to ignore their stress upon the loving desire for change of heart in the opponent is to misrepresent the rationale of the present movement. But where is the structural guarantee that this relationship of motive and techniques is not accidental and coincidental rather than necessary and required?

Is brainwashing, for example, an emerging expression of nonviolent coercion in demonic form? Brainwashing uses both the threat of privation and the promise of reward to undercut the moral resistance of its victims. In this respect it is similar to other forms of coercion even though it is not overtly violent. Thus far brainwashing has been initiated only in situations created by victory with conventional violence, but is this the only possible condition under which the techniques can be employed? Can they be used in circumstances where violence has not first made victims? How different is brainwashing from manipulative propaganda, from certain kinds of advertising that force emotional responses without appealing to deliberate and free judgments? The answers to these questions have not yet been made, but even the questions give us pause to wonder about such issues.

To define struggle with a scope so broad that conquest of nature and coercion in war are made aspects of a common genus, together with other types of conflict in the life of man, can be justified by the fact that strife and striving are present in all the realities that have been described. While these elements of strife and striving constitute a common feature, the problems they create may appear in different ways in the different forms of struggle that have been discussed. There is yet another unifying element, so obvious we might even fail to mention it. All the forms of struggle that have been discussed involve the human self as either the maker or victim of conflict. The nature of this self and its possible relationships to struggle must next become the focus of our attention.

II

THE SELF IN RELATION TO CONFLICT: THE MIRROR AND AGENT OF STRUGGLE

THE use of the term "self" has gradually overshadowed the use of the term "soul" in many fields of human discourse. A past generation was raised on William Ernest Henley's *Invictus* and spoke of itself as the captain of its soul. A present generation, no less aware of the fact of struggle in human life and its bitter trials for the individual, seeks through thought and action to find "authentic selfhood."

There are not many thinkers today who would defend the thesis advanced by the indomitable Henley:

> It matters not how strait the gate,
> How charged with punishments the scroll,
> I am the master of my fate:
> I am the captain of my soul.

Perhaps Henley does not really mean that the fortunes of life have no impact upon him. Perhaps Henley's use of a term which for many people signifies a special and extra-temporal entity that is largely oblivious to circumstance gives the wrong impression. No man can undergo the buffetings and tensions of life without consequences for his selfhood. Most of us will settle for a selfhood that stands firm, though not quite unchanged, amidst the costly and troublesome experiences of human existence.

24

The preference among psychologists for the term "self" is easily understood. The term "self" can do the work of the term "soul" without raising the specter of a psychosomatic schizoid. The sociologist will prefer the word because he is interested in the relationship of the individual to his environment and understands the effects of that environment upon the selfhood of those who are subject to it. The clinical observer wants to know what strains and stresses impinge upon the life of the individual with whom he deals, and the student of social patterns is frequently concerned about the kinds of personal responses that are demanded of individuals by the situations to which they are related. Moreover, he will want to know the kinds of structures created by certain types of individuals. The theologian should be interested in what both groups have to say and their reasons for saying it.

We can be glad, then, to find that the use of the term "self" is not only acceptable to the great majority of contemporary theologians but is actually defended by them as true to the Biblical understanding of man and his place within the world. The term "self" (or "self-in-relation") fittingly denotes the proper object of psychological inquiry, sociological analysis, and theological reflection. The man in the pew may still echo the formulations of the evangelist and speak about the salvation of his soul, but the theologians are writing about *The Self and the Dramas of History* and *Christian Understandings of Selfhood*.

But if man cannot be understood as a soul alone, neither can he be understood merely as a psychosomatic entity in time and space. In adopting the term "self" for use in discussing the nature of man the theological world is not intending to surrender the case to a naturalistic metaphysic. The self is said by many theologians to transcend its own position in space and time, to stand apart and above itself and to ask who and what it is in itself. It can even see itself doing this and thus enjoys the transcendence of its own transcendence. Each self does this in a way that is unique to itself, not in radical discontinuity with other selves yet with an integrity and special quality reserved to it alone.

It is possible to use the term self-transcendence to refer to a kind of objective look at oneself that can be accounted for within the limits of the natural order. This use of the term better fits psychological discussions than theological affirmations. In using the experience of self-transcendence to indicate a theory of the self that is metaphysical in its implications the theologians are indicating their own convictions concerning the ultimate character of man. Speaking of these matters, Lewis J. Sherrill has said:

> Self-transcendence has at least two aspects which are of special importance in the line of thought we are following. For one thing, self-transcendence means that the human creature, who is in nature and subject to nature, is able also at the same time to transcend nature. He dwells in the finite world of nature which cradles him. And yet he dwells also in a realm of spirit (*The Gift of Power*, p. 10. The Macmillan Company, 1955. Used by permission.)

Sherrill includes in the realm of spirit those many aspects of human thought which have no tangible reality yet clearly influence the actions and behavior of men. Qualities like "justice, equality, liberty, democracy, righteousness, love and hate, decency and fair play" are certainly real even though they are not physical and corporeal. The self is similarly constituted, and though it belongs in one sense to the realm of spirit, it has a real impact upon the world about it. "Spirit is the intangible totality which the self is, and at the same time is the forthgoing of that intangible totality toward and into others." (*Ibid.*, p. 11.)

The spirit of man must not be elevated to the transcendent capacity alone any more than it should be reduced to a merely somatic impact upon nature. Erich Frank has rightly suggested that man "is always more than he is able to comprehend of himself" (*Philosophical Understanding and Religious Truth*, p. 8. Oxford University Press, 1945. Used by permission). By this, Frank means that man is more than intellect alone and cannot be understood solely in theoretical terms. As a philosopher, Frank comes to the conclusion that man comes to know himself in the dimensions of existence that involve struggle and suffering, for it is at these points that he encounters his own limitations and comes to recognize them. For Frank the struggle of life, the effort to secure justice and order in a world of conflicting vitalities, the resistance of the individual to his own abstract reason, all witness more eloquently and profoundly to the nature of man than the detached logic of speculative understanding. Even speculative thought itself becomes the occasion of conflict:

Truth cannot be found solely through the logical harmony of our own thought. We must contend with the truths of others, which in themselves may be equally logical and harmonious and yet are contradictory to what we think to be true. The final antinomy that appears in all philosophical discussions results from the contradictory character of our fundamental rational principles. This dialectical character of philosophical thought cannot be explained simply by the subjective limitations of our intellect, but must have its origin in the nature of reality itself, which everywhere manifests a tension of opposing forces. Therefore, even philosophizing means strife. (*Ibid.*, pp. 14 f.)

The contrast between a view that finds thought to be an extended version of life, including the element of conflict, and a view that hopes by means of thought to overcome the antagonisms of life, is not to be lightly ignored. In many academic institutions the vocal praises rendered the detached and objective mind are related to the hope that rational understanding can remake social realities if only it is applied with sufficient earnestness. But when the same advocates of the rational approach do business with each other in the conflicting vitalities of faculty relationships the objectivity is hard to find. Under the best conditions it consists of a tolerable politeness that accepts with good spirit the outcome of group process; under less favorable conditions it is superseded by rancor and jealousy.

Alexander Miller has wisely insisted that man cannot know himself by introspection alone. His selfhood is not only pulse but commitment. It is to be known through encounter and involvement with life and not by standing aside in detached inquiry. Miller argues that its experiences define the location (or status) of the self rather than its inner qualities, and that self-knowledge consists of relational knowledge concerning where we come from and what we strive after rather than the analytical knowledge of our innermost being. (*The Man in the Mirror: Studies in the Christian Understanding of Selfhood,* Ch. I.)

If Miller is right, as indeed he is, then struggle is one of the arenas of life in which knowledge of the self is obtained. I know more about myself when I see how I react in tension than when I answer application forms calling for a fifty-word summary of my attitude toward life. If I lose my temper under pressure or retreat from reality when the going gets difficult, then I must confess to a different kind of selfhood than if I react to tensions with poise and self-control. Many a meek young lad, deemed by his fellow youth as bookish or retiring, left behind in the contests for popularity, never a hero at the football stadium, has proved to be made of stern stuff in later years. In situations of temptation that call for integrity or in situations of danger that call for bravery the mild and retiring self may outshine the braggart.

One cannot count on this result any more than he can depend on the opposite. The football hero may become the brave warrior, and the meek and bookish student may be crushed by the rigors of later life. There is mystery and unpredictability here that even psychological tests do not entirely fathom and probably never will. The freedom of the self ranges too widely to enable us to reduce to certainty all predictions concerning its possible behavior. The self that reacts with cowardice in one situation may be so repulsed by its own behavior that in the next instance it will partially or entirely reverse the pattern of response. Sensing the mystery of selfhood, Reinhold Niebuhr has asserted "that there are heights and depths of human selfhood which are beyond any system of rational intelligibility, but not beyond the comprehension of faith and hope." (*The Self and the Dramas of History*, p. 239. Charles Scribner's Sons, 1955. Used by permission.) Knowledge of the self obtained from observing its behavior in conflict may be sounder knowledge than what can be obtained through introspection, but even here we see through a glass darkly.

Perhaps the difficulty with our thinking about the self is our preoccupation with determining what we are rather than what we do. Socrates enjoined his hearers to "know thyself." Descartes re-emphasized the centrality of the self by founding his thought on the certainty of its doubting. Even those approaches that would define the self by reference to its struggles rather than its essential being are still apt to be concerned with the abstract definition of what constitutes selfhood. John Macmurray has made a thorough critique of this posture, a posture of thought he feels is deeply rooted in the entire history of the West. (We might add parenthetically that much thought in the East is similarly concerned with the detached quality of being rather than the dynamic quality of acting.) Macmurray is convinced that this error appears, not only in the traditional philosophies of Western civilization, but in the two most popular schools of contemporary philosophical reflection. Neither existentialism nor positivism has removed the self from the central role of *subject*. In the first, the individual is isolated; in the second, the individual is abstracted into a theoretical knower. Hence "modern philosophy is characteristically *egocentric*." (*The Self as Agent*, p. 31. Harper & Brothers, 1957. Used by permission.)

Macmurray puts it even more elaborately:

In actuality, the solitary self can only mean the Self in reflection, self-isolated from the world, withdrawn into itself. This is the Self in self-negation, the negative aspect of selfhood, or the Self as subject. The standpoint of the solitary self, if that Self is considered to be actual or existent, is therefore necessarily the theoretical standpoint. (*Ibid.*, pp. 14 f.)

Perhaps we shy from Macmurray's radical insistence upon a philosophy of action rather than of contemplation because we instinctively feel that much of our behavior is determined by subrational considerations, and are loathe to admit the fact. This need not imply that such considerations are any less worthy or dependable than actions rooted in the supposedly pure ground of reflective reason. Who will not trust the man of long-developed inner character whose very fabric of selfhood is endowed with a quality of integrity and dependability that is transparent to all who know him? Many of us trust such a person more implicitly than we will trust a brilliant and flashy young genius whose "rational analyses" startle the understanding yet defy prediction. The cultural tradition of a people frequently determines their behavior as much or more than does their articulation of the moral issues, and this fact is embarrassing to a philosophical outlook that makes analytical reason the explanation and arbiter of all things. When those of us who engage in speculative thought act in the normal course of daily life it is hard to tell us apart from men of more practical pursuits—except perhaps by the fact that many eggheads are helpless with a monkey wrench or gullible when reading a price tag.

There has been a great deal of interest on the part of many students of human behavior about the relationship of selfhood and struggle, but not all such interest bridges the gap about which Macmurray complains. Many students of the human psyche employ the terms "conflict" and "struggle" to speak of the strife and striving that takes place within the individual himself. The spirit can be torn asunder by internal conflict. Those skilled in such matters render much needed service to their fellowmen when they bring internal conflict to tolerable limits. Without discounting their work we are concerned about another kind of problem. There is a relationship between inner conflict within the individual and social consequences within the group of which he is a part. The individual is both affected by and in turn affects his environment. Less by intention than by default, much of the psychological and psychoanalytical discussion of selfhood has tacitly assumed a conception of wholeness as something sought and developed on the largely personal level of experience, and sometimes sought for it in essentially individualistic terms. The relevance of spiritual wholeness to the discussion of social issues and realities has never been denied, yet it has frequently been ignored.

In other discussions the social situation has been considered merely as the extended case of the personal one. Reinhold Niebuhr has observed the oversimplifications that flow from the tendency of the behavioral sciences to deal with social realities in the same terms as they deal with personal conflicts.

It is certainly not relevant to deal with the monumental collective egoism of nations, compounded of many genuinely historical cumulations; of illusion, and power lusts, as if they were merely the aggregate of individual "aggressiveness." Thus a discipline, which has proved therapeutically efficient in dealing with pathological states of individuals, has been betrayed into the inanity of speculating whether the Germans, Russians and Japanese could be cured of their "aggressiveness" by a sufficiently wide application of psycho-therapy. (Niebuhr, *op. cit.*, p. 10.)

The failure to bring psychological thought into working relationship with social thought may possibly be explained in yet another way. Christian social thought has moved away from an emphasis upon personal virtues and the cultivation of individual attitudes of charity and openness at exactly the time when the development of behavioral understandings has been making rapid strides. Emphasis upon the structural arrangements of a just order have taken priority over the cultivation of personal virtues in the same period when the attention devoted to the inward qualities of selfhood by students of the human personality might have made a contribution to the amelioration of social conflict. The overly simplified answers proposed by some psychologists are one source of a split; an inhospitality on the part of some Christian social thought to such explorations may be another.

This divorce between social ethical thought and personality theory bears closer scrutiny. We are told, for example, that we must not allow ourselves to decide the qualifications of political candidates on the basis of personal charm and polish of manner. Even the moral integrity of candidates is less crucial to the consequences that flow from their election than the kinds of policies they advocate and the purposes that they will seek to advance through their exercise of public office. But must we not recognize that the purposes men seek to advance are indicative of their selfhood at least as much, and probably more, than the kind of etiquette they have mastered? Though great harm can follow from an overly simplified or sentimentalized judgment of candidates on purely personal qualities, the contributions of the self cannot be ignored in the evaluation of men for public trust. Selfhood affects not only minor decisions but the ways in which men come to decisions on major policy issues.

At the risk of smashing fragile eggs we are bold to draw a comparison at this point between the personalities of Harry S. Truman and John F. Kennedy. Each of these two men has stood on essentially the same policy program for the presidential office, but their style of personal leadership is quite different. Truman's outbursts of petty frankness stand in sharp contrast to Kennedy's suave poise. Those who grew sour about Truman, or were merely looking for a ready excuse to criticize the man, seized upon his indignities as the proof of his unfitness for public office. In many cases such criticism sprang from bitter partisanship and thus needs to be discounted, but there were other cases in which a public grew disgusted with the lack of dignity and let its disgust overshadow its judgments about policy matters. It may even be that Truman brought defeat to his own policy position by alienating a margin of voters who put personal dignity above policy advocacy in choosing a candidate for the presidential office. Conversely, Kennedy's popularity rose during his initial months in the White House, at least in part because his poise and dignity commended itself to even a group of voters who had not cast their ballots for his election. This difference may or may not significantly determine the kind of record each makes during his tenure of office, but it will no doubt affect the kind of image recorded in the annals of future history. This difference would be greatly magnified if, in addition to differences on the personality level, sharp differences existed between these two men on policy issues as well.

If the nature of selfhood affects the ways in which men deal with personal behavior and public trust, we should examine the following interpretation of Biblical thought with a cautious eye:

The apostolic summary of the whole law in the love of neighbor, the close connection between love of neighbor and love of God in Jesus' summary, the prophetic demand for justice and mercy, and the concern of the Ten Commandments with conduct that affects the companion all underscore . . . [the point that ethics concerns the treatment of the neighbor]. Its significance appears further in the fact that none of these summaries indicates any interest in virtues apart from their place in one's relation to other persons. There is no demand in any of them for truthfulness as such but only for truthfulness toward the neighbor; there is not even a demand for love as such. No action is considered right simply on account of its effects on the self. (Waldo Beach and H. Richard Niebuhr, *Christian Ethics—Sources of the Living Tradition,* p. 16. Copyright, 1955, by The Ronald Press Company. Used by permission.)

This quotation is right in its insistence that the neighbor's good has priority in the determination of Christian moral decision. It could be wrongly read as implying that the attitudes and loyalties of the self have no bearing upon the way the neighbor's good is treated. Incidentally, and perhaps not so incidentally at that, the Beatitudes are not so easily encompassed by this characterization of Biblical morality. Kierkegaard is not the only Christian theologian to have read moral obligation in the vertical terms implied by purity of heart.

The analysis that follows concerns the relationship of the individual to those forms of struggle that involve his selfhood with its environment. Its orientation is sociological rather than psychological insofar as its main concern is about the consequences for society that flow from the different ways in which individuals deal with the element of strife in human life. However, it is not unconcerned about the ways in which struggle affects the selfhood of those who are involved in it, and would not shy from the implication that the spiritual quality of participation is quite as pertinent for religious understandings as the objective social positions advocated by an individual. Our plea is basically that these problems not be split apart and that the two approaches not be considered mutually exclusive. We cannot settle for either side of a false antinomy.

It must be granted that these observations are made from within the theological thought world. Perhaps others have had more to say about the relationship of personal selfhood and social consequences than have the authors familiar to this writer. Moreover, we are speaking of a general tendency to keep these fields of concern apart and not of an iron curtain between them. Bridges have been built across the gulf. We must not overlook studies like the brilliant, yet highly impressionistic, observations on the kinds of people that join mass movements that we find in Eric Hoffer's *The True Believer*. Social psychology has something to contribute to our insight. Even so, most Christian social ethics speak of one kind of problem, and the literature dealing with the relationship of psychoanalytical insights to the Christian understanding of man deals with another.

The enterprise we have in mind depends upon a view of the self that sees it as both mirror and agent of social process and not as mirror alone. The self is an actor in a drama not entirely of its own choosing yet certainly not beyond its genuine ability to influence. The lines of the drama may be written elsewhere but they are performed on this stage and are given the inflections, tone, and implications that the actors choose for them at the moment of performance. The idea of the self-as-agent does not presuppose omnipotence over the events of history, but it does suggest that man can choose whether he is dragged, he shuffles, or he marches along the way. The case for human responsibility is not tied to the idea of unlimited freedom; any reasonable margin of choice calls for it.

The theologian will finally insist that the self be understood, not only in relationship to its environment and in terms of its attitude about it, but in terms of its relationship to judgment and grace. These terms are used to indicate respectively the negative and positive dimensions of the healing relationship between God and man.

Both judgment and grace conjure up largely individualistic images in the public mind. Judgment is taken to mean the final appearance of the lonesome soul before the pearly gates, and even after a long and deliberate explanation of judgment as the scrutiny of man's present life in the light of God's holiness the majority of hearers will still think of judgment in purely finalistic and individualistic terms! This is the more discouraging because the corporate dimensions of judgment and the relationship between judgment and man's social situation have received tremendous emphasis in the writings of theologians in all ages, and particularly so in the past few decades. War has been interpreted as God's judgment upon the nations, and social unrest in the underdeveloped areas of the world has frequently been interpreted as the consequence of our failure to be concerned about the neighbor.

The self understands itself—but even more, comes to itself—when it confronts its own limitations and shortcomings in the experience of failure. This is what happened in the case of the prodigal son, who might not have returned to his father had his flight from home ended in worldly success. Nor is all judgment followed by grace. It is reported that the navigator who gave the signals for the atomic bombings of Nagasaki and Hiroshima was so haunted by feelings of guilt that he could not sleep for years afterward. He tried to bury his guilt in drink and has since spent time in a mental hospital. While it is unwise to consider that a single event can alone account for all subsequent behavior, there is no denying the fact that conflict can thrust men into circumstances that expose the limited adequacy of their own virtue. It is frequently in conflict that we come to realize how unprofitable we are as servants of the good and how clearly we make our own contributions to the sickness of the body politic.

But if the public mind conjures up largely individualistic images about judgment, it would seem that it can arrive at practically nothing else when thinking about grace. The relationship between selfhood and salvation in individual terms so far outshadows the attention paid to the role of grace in social processes that, with a few important exceptions, the theologians are also a party to the process. Rightly anxious to avoid the identification of any historical accomplishment with the ultimate healing activity of God, we have increasingly shied away from any strong affirmations about the way God's grace operates in history. Consequently, salvation is a term whose connotations are largely formed for us by the highly individualistic and otherworldly branches of Christianity. The self looks forward to the final encounter with its Maker as a decisive payoff at the end of its own earthly pilgrimage. No wonder Alexander Miller cried in near-despair:

I confess that I am bound to think the incorrigible individualism of the times is the source of most bedevilment in matters of faith. It is compensated for, but not corrected, by endless *joining;* it is not corrected because on the whole the joining is done to cover an anxious individualism, and for "what can be got out of" the group. It is, I suppose, a characteristic of fallen human nature; but it is enhanced by the American ethos. The world is my oyster; and everything that is proposed to me, including education and religion, is to be tested by whether or not it helps me to open it. (*The Man in the Mirror,* p. 166. Copyright © 1958, by Alexander Miller. Reprinted by permission of Doubleday & Company, Inc.)

The obvious question on the border line between the self and its society is the moral one, and this bears close affinities to the problem of judgment and grace. Should men engage in struggle, and if so, under what conditions?

From what perspective are they to arrive at answers to such a query? Why is it not enough simply to affirm or to deny the rightful place of struggle in human life and men's place within struggle itself? Why do the moral problems related to the struggle of nature seem as minimal as those related to warfare seem pressing?

But there are other problems on the border line between the self and its role in struggle. The self is a thinking, willing being that builds loyalties and creates hopes, directs its action toward the expression of these loyalties and lives in response to all that takes place around it. Hence, the meaning of struggle for selfhood and the kinds of loyalties it creates beg for understanding along with the problem of its rightful conduct. In the first chapter we outlined the kinds of struggle in which the self can be engaged; in the next chapter we shall look carefully at the kinds of reactions the self may have as a result of such involvement. We shall find that the evaluations of struggle are as diverse as its forms.

III

THE UNPLEASANT, IMMORAL, AND IDOLATROUS: CRITICISMS OF STRUGGLE

MEN become involved in struggle for many reasons, and their attitudes toward involvement are compounded of many factors. There is a strange repulsion about struggle, but also an allurement. Struggle frequently entails the contradiction of moral ideals, yet may also be the means of defending cherished values. It can be unpleasant and glorious, even at the same time. It can cause men to perform barbarisms yet also bring forth nobility of character. In the strange paradox of fascination and fear, repulsion and attraction, moral compromise and heroic grandeur, men are drawn into struggle—sometimes to their destruction and at other times to their personal enrichment. Ray Ginger has indicated the complex human reactions to struggle with the imaginary musings of an individual citizen considering whether or not his nation should enter a war:

Should we enter the war? Well, this country is the best there is, and I want it to be the strongest there is, and the price of corn would go up, and Germans are no good, but even Germans are human, and the Bible says thou shalt not kill, and my three sons would have to go in the Army, and I'd have a terrible time hiring hands, and gas for the truck would be hard to get. (*Six Days or Forever?* p. 223. Reprinted by permission of the Beacon Press, © 1958 by Ray Ginger.)

The title for this chapter contains negative terms related to various criticisms of struggle. In their evaluations of struggle men usually first consider what is wrong with it, and we have followed this inclination. The criticism that follows is intended to look at the false uses of struggle rather than to condemn it as such. Struggle is not altogether bad or necessarily to be eliminated from human life. Politics can provide men with the zest and zeal to live despite its many agonies; even war can help some men to discover a selfhood they may rightly cherish even though its major effects are disastrous. It is legitimate to consider struggle as an indication of man's need for grace yet at the same time to recognize it as a reality through which grace may operate. Much depends upon the manner in which conflict is embraced.

There is an esthetic dislike of many ingredients of struggle in the reactions of most men. We do not like to face a formidable opponent; we hate to battle enemies with guns or neighbors with wits. We resent the privations, restrictions, upsets, and sacrifices of war. We are made nervous by the uncertainties of competitive plays for power and privilege. Nobody likes gas rationing, conscription laws, high taxes for weapons and support of allies. To hold both temper and tongue in the face of insults, to entertain potential business "contacts" when little common sharing of ideas or interests occurs, to keep an eye peeled for the advance of the contending challenger—all set the nerves on edge and may destroy the integrity of the self. Even the conquest of nature can be a grim business: labor in the laboratory, fruitless bad starts, dead ends, or successes that come without proper acknowledgment or recognition.

It is more than the fear of danger that makes war unpleasant. It is more than the fear of going down in defeat that makes the daily rat race unpalatable. The fruitless boredom of drudgery plagues every type of struggle—from the military guard watch to the scientific experiment. Even the intellectual life, presumably the life of excitement and vision, was aptly described by the writer of Ecclesiastes as "a weariness of the flesh." Recruits in a drill platoon and high school boys in a mathematics class would gladly exchange their places, for neither at the moment likes the situation at hand. The drill sergeant is often hated, and likewise the math instructor, because they represent an enforced involvement with routine. Struggle is difficult and even unpleasant, and those who enforce it upon us are symbols of the system that grinds men into the obedient submission to the routine without which they cannot succeed in their calling.

There can be born from this dislike of struggle an effort to escape from life. When this occurs in extreme forms, neuroses and psychoses result, and the self retreats to a dream state. But the dislike of struggle has consequences even within the sphere of normal behavior, and when it is dominant, social evils can arise in addition to personal maladjustment. People who dislike controversy are usually inept at politics, and by withdrawing from the unpleasant mess leave the field to the less sensitive. Many systems of injustice are created by people who prefer serenity to social turmoil and who accept benevolent tyranny with its security and calm rather than fight for democratic processes with their upsets and turmoil. In wartime the scorn and ridicule hurled upon the slacker makes withdrawal from coercive conflict on esthetic grounds highly unlikely. In other kinds of struggle, however, we still accept and even admire the nonparticipant, the political independent, the faithful and kindly toolmaker, or the janitor.

It is perhaps in the effort to counteract the repulsive elements in struggle that men try to glorify it. Wars are pictured as opportunities for heroism; competitive economy is a chance for the individual to prove his worth; the work of the scientist is romanticized by magazine advertisements. It is a sober, yet a worthy, exercise in reflection to stand at a post office and contemplate the appeals of the recruiting posters. Not only do they seem to ignore the political need for seeking men to bear arms, but they exhibit curious differences between the services as to the type of glory men most want. Perhaps Eric Hoffer is right when he observes that:

The indispensability of play-acting in the grim business of dying and killing is particularly evident in the case of armies. Their uniforms, flags, emblems, parades, music, and elaborate etiquette and ritual are designed to separate the soldier from his flesh-and-blood self and mask the overwhelming reality of life and death. (Eric Hoffer, *The True Believer,* p. 66. Harper & Brothers, 1951. Used by permission.)

Not all the glory of the military life is to be scorned. Military training is ultimately directed toward competence in the destruction of an adversary, but life in the military has its pageantry and sense of belonging to a social unit. Training in a cadet corps can have derivative benefits that even pacifists can admire. Neat uniforms and polished shoes and even the polite use of submissive language all help to take the rough edges off the rugged individual. The sense of belonging to a community can be more real in a regiment than it is in many a church cell. Harry Emerson Fosdick, in his later years a convinced and vocal pacifist, recalls with satisfaction time he spent as a boy in a cadet organization sponsored by the local unit of the National Guard.

But struggle cannot be justified by citing the possible glory any more than it can be rejected because of its unpleasant qualities. It is possible to escape from life by glorifying struggle just as readily as by being overwhelmed by its distasteful features. To glorify struggle because some aspects of it do call forth heroism and qualities of discipline is as false as to withdraw from struggle simply on the grounds that it is too sordid and uncouth for decent men. The slacker is a proper object of public scorn; the flag-waver ought also to be. The ill-adjusted Bohemian type may refuse to struggle because he wishes to escape; other ill-adjusted types may join the Foreign Legion for essentially the same reasons.

To withdraw from any form of struggle because it is unpleasant is to give up the battle or forfeit the contest. It is to invite defeat at the hands of any group that chooses to create a fuss. There are few victories in human life that are universally hailed with enthusiastic acceptance. Effective political struggle may entail a challenge to the existing order and be followed by bitter attacks upon those who undertake it. It may involve unity of purpose with repulsive groups and reap the fruits of enmity as well as gratitude. Every reaction that puts a premium on politeness alone is open to challenge by those who can make people cringe merely by threatening the calm of the existing order. Every prophetic movement that puts a premium on righteousness and justice will be resisted, scourged, and dishonored by at least a large segment of the society in which it works. It may be hated because it disturbs the euphoria of even those it seeks to serve. Social change is not effected by polite men working with kid gloves through a process of gradual moral evolution. It is born of struggle and reared in tension. It is worth the effort to keep struggle within limits and the tensions below the explosion point, but to expect immunity from the agony attending social change is to be tempted to have no part in bringing it about.

But it is possible to regard struggle as unworthy and wrong on ethical rather than esthetic grounds. Any process that depends for its final success upon the intended destruction of the opponent is subject to judgment on moral grounds. From within such a judgment it is the immoral rather than the unpleasant elements in struggle that tempt men to reject its use. It is never pleasant "to beat out the brains" of an opponent, and neither is it good to do so. The moral refusal to be party to the process is far sounder than is a mere esthetic withdrawal.

But though moral reasons for a refusal to become involved in struggle are more adequate than merely esthetic ones, they are also much less common. Conscientious objection to the duties of military life has remained a minority movement in Western culture ever since the days of Constantine. Its dishonored and disinherited state has kept it from becoming a haven for those whose objection to struggle is merely a desire to avoid the unpleasant. Whatever may be our judgment concerning the pragmatic wisdom of conscientious objection, its ethical judgment is sound. Any process that seeks the destruction of the opponent is fundamentally wrong by any ultimate standard of goodness.

To forget or to obscure this judgment under any circumstances is to lose some of the sensitivity that belongs to men of high moral insight and profound religious conviction. There is a genuine and vital role for the conscientious objector—the role of witness to the fundamental moral problems involved in struggle, and especially in struggle of the coercive type. Unless some men exercise this witness in a world dominated by bitter hostilities and the wanton use of power something vital in the religious heritage of many traditions will be eclipsed. Love of neighbor, kindness to enemies, and willingness to suffer rather than to inflict pain belong to the grand vision of high religion. To lose sight of the vision or to reject it as wrong and sentimental is to court the destruction of the moral ideal. The demonic urges of men bent on hate and destruction far exceed in fury and in scope the tooth-and-claw realities of the animal world.

The intended destruction of an opponent is most obvious and most furious in the case of coercive struggle, though in the next chapter we shall argue that it is a common feature of all struggle. It is therefore understandable that conscientious objection should most commonly be made against military service. From time to time and place to place, however, we find analagous withdrawal from participation in competitive struggles, or at least those forms of competitive struggle that grant status to those who climb on the backs of underlings. Roman Catholic monasticism is a viable alternative to life in suburbia with its scrambles and pressures, and while the possible reasons for entering the monastic life are complex and varied, negatively considered monasticism can be embraced because of the desire to escape the moral compromises that attend competitive existence. Ascetic monasticism, however, creates the struggle to conquer nature in a more intense form, and it is hard to see how it can be considered as a means of escaping all forms of conscious striving.

Small communities of voluntary membership created in the effort to develop a noncompetitive life have appeared in our day, some in Europe, some in the United States. Small in number and limited in scope these communities seek a style of living in which the element of competition within their fellowship is minimized. Frequently agrarian or manual in their economic base, they accept the legitimacy of struggle against nature but reject the legitimacy of struggle for economic privilege or social position. They may or may not take a position of objection to coercive struggle, though the individual membership is commonly recruited from those who have highly developed moral scruples about participation in armed conflict. The acceptance of voluntary poverty, or the life of minimal subsistence, is a symbol in such groups of the rejection of the struggle for status and success. Hence, the *Rule of Taizé* says: "The poor of the Gospel learn to live without assurance for tomorrow, in joyful confidence that all will be provided. . . .The spirit of poverty is to live in the cheerfulness of today." (P. 54.)

These groups play the same roles as witness to the dangers of plenty as the conscientious objector plays to the inhumanity and moral compromise involved in the resort to violence. Men may choose to draw a line in these matters at any point without being accused of bad faith, and sheer consistency is neither possible nor demanded. The economic position of many conscientious objectors to war is ample evidence that they have not turned their back upon the world of competitive financial gain; the hard field work of the Amish farmer is evidence that he has not rejected the effort to conquer nature. It is possible to select the kinds of struggle one will embrace and reject —the selection being dependent upon the vocation of the given individual who makes it.

Such decisions as men draw in these cases are never absolute, nor can they be the final measure of religious adequacy. If they are drawn with finality at any point, a tentative and limited (and even subjective) moral judgment is given excessive weight and final ultimacy. If taken as a measure of goodness rather than as a worthy witness, the position of the objector to struggle misplays itself. It frequently becomes the occasion of self-righteousness and self-esteem, in which its understanding of virtue is paraded as greater than that of other men. When this occurs the entire spiritual situation of the vocational witness is altered and a new struggle develops between the self-righteous rejectors of struggle and its self-righteous affirmers. Debates between pacifists and nonpacifists frequently grow bitter because each side feels it is right and the other side is wrong. Charity and love have not always been the exclusive property of one side in such debates, if indeed they have been the property of either!

This argument presupposes a conception of ethical decision based upon the vocation of the individual in his responsibility to God. It does not insist that a particular moral judgment about struggle is universally binding upon every man. It opens the door for individual decision and is relativistic about the content of such decision. The point of reference is to God and not to a categorical imperative. But the relativism is qualified by the argument that follows, wherein we hold that the way in which decisions about participation in struggle are made and employed has as much bearing upon our relationship to other men as the contents of the decisions themselves. It is possible either to embrace or to reject struggle in a mood and manner that does as much harm or as much good as does the decision whether or not to do so. There are conscientious participants and conscientious objectors to struggle, both of whose moral sensitivity we might wish to become universal. Conversely, there are objectors and participants whose behavior is the bane of corporate existence.

If this is so, then we must look at the ways in which struggle can be embraced with moral sensitivity as well as outline the socially harmful ways in which it is affirmed. Some observers discount the possibility of an authentic moral justification for coercion. They are convinced that moral rationalizations for resort to arms or appeals for political support are nothing but the cloaked self-interest of the participants. Without advocating such an extreme view Herbert Butterfield has nevertheless observed that claims concerning the moral justification for war cannot be taken uncritically:

The crudities of popular ethics render the political exploitation of morality a comparatively easy matter. By making

consistent use of methods that were developed in the West—
by turning the weapons of democracy against democracy itself—the Communists have brought to a climax the use of
moral indignation as a weapon of power politics. (*International Conflict in the Twentieth Century: A Christian View*,
pp. 23 f. Harper & Brothers, 1960. Used by permission.)

Pacifists deny that conflict can ever be conducted in a
moral manner because they feel that all coercive struggle
is morally questionable. Cynics deny that conflict can
ever be conducted in a moral manner because they suspect
every moral claim of being the rationalization of self-
interest. They make a curious set of bedfellows, though
they seldom if ever acknowledge their similarity. If we do
well to remember the witness of the pacifist to the moral
compromise of war, we should do well to make at least a
provisional allowance for the insight of the cynic. Both
Machiavelli's prince and Nietzsche's superman were created by their authors as men who use the moral pose of the
fighter with consummate skill and total beguilement. The
hero must appear good even though he is a scoundrel! As
a warning against sentimentality the cynic's view has a
place, but in the last analysis it obscures the genuine ambiguities in the relationship between morality and struggle
by giving way to a one-sided evaluation.

It is increasingly common to make a distinction between
justifiable coercion, symbolized by the just war, and the
moral crusade. In the former, coercion is embraced as a
means to accomplish some moral good and remains under
the scrutiny of moral judgments fairly acknowledged by
its pursuers; in the latter, coercion becomes almost an end
in itself and subordinates all other values to its successful
conduct. In succinct compass Roland Bainton has observed:

Broadly speaking, three attitudes to war and peace were to
appear in the Christian ethic: pacifism, the just war, and the

crusade. Chronologically they have emerged in just this order. The early church was pacifist to the time of Constantine. Then, partly as a result of the close association of Church and state under this emperor and partly by reason of the threat of barbarian invasions, Christians in the fourth and fifth centuries took over from the classical world the doctrine of the just war, whose object should be to vindicate justice and restore peace. The just war had to be fought under the authority of the state and must observe a code of good faith and humanity. The Christian elements added by Augustine were that the motive must be love and that monks and priests were to be exempted. The crusade arose in the high Middle Ages, a holy war fought under the auspices of the Church or of some inspired religious leader, not on behalf of justice conceived in terms of life and property, but on behalf of an ideal, the Christian faith. Since the enemy was without the pale, the code tended to break down. (*Christian Attitudes Toward War and Peace,* p. 14. Abingdon Press, 1960. Used by permission.)

Paul Ramsey urges us to consider the positive Christian obligation to embrace the conduct of justifiable war. He argues that participation is demanded of Christians because love for neighbor involves them "in maintaining the organized social and political life in which all men live" (*War and the Christian Conscience,* p. xvii. Duke University Press, 1961). At the same time Ramsey insists that such an obligation entails severe self-limitations over the manner in which coercion may be used, for example, the prohibition of mass killing of noncombatants.

Ramsey raises a strong voice in a strange land, for the common moral judgments of struggle come in terms of blacks and whites, demanding unqualified rejection of its use or unqualified acceptance. If men find the destructive intentions of struggle morally wrong, they become pacifists; if they find the use of struggle valuable in defense of cherished values, they baptize the instrument with holy sanction. When such sanction is prompted by religious motives the crusade results. "One observes how ill fared the code for humane conduct required by the just war when the conflict became a crusade. War is more humane when God is left out of it." (Roland Bainton, *op. cit.*, p. 49.)

From the great zeal of the crusade come many of the worst chapters in mankind's saga, for the crusader is less flexible and tolerant than the policeman, and the inquisitor is more ruthless than the soldier. But crusades do not necessarily have overt religious sanction. They arise whenever the conduct of war becomes an end in itself. The historian Herbert Butterfield is not far from the truth in the observation that

the greatest menace to our civilization today is the conflict between giant organized systems of self-righteousness—each system only too delighted to find that the other is wicked—each only too glad that the sins give it the pretext for still deeper hatred and animosity. The effect of the whole situation is barbarizing, since both sides take the wickedness of the other as the pretext for insults, atrocities, and loathing; and each side feels that its own severities are not vicious at all, but simply punitive acts and laudable measures of judgment. (*Christianity, Diplomacy, and War*, p. 43. The Epworth Press, Publishers, London, n.d.)

As an esthetic problem, struggle presents the ambiguity between unpleasantness and glory. As a moral problem it presents the mixture of immorality and the defense of righteousness. Struggle can also be evaluated as a religious problem since it involves loyalties and commitments and may even become the object of commitment. In many human conflicts struggle itself becomes as important as the purposes for which it is undertaken, and men are judged by their compatriots even more by their willingness to struggle than in terms of the ends for which they wage it.

The allegiance of many voters to their political party must be understood as a pseudoreligious phenomenon.

Loyal to party because of parental heritage or economic conditioning, many voters ignore those social and political goals for which the party of their loyalty is supposed to stand. They are Republicans because their fathers are, or because their great-grandfathers voted for Lincoln; they are Democrats because Jefferson was or because Republicans belong north of the Mason-Dixon line. They are Republicans because all the office staff, as well as the bosses, are; Democrats because they belong to social groups in which their peers think highly of New Deals and New Frontiers.

Allegiance to party can persist despite policy positions at sharp variance with conviction. Southern Democrats have long supported governmental policies that they intensely dislike because their loyalty to party is even stronger than their insistence upon a particular kind of public policy. To be sure, there are problems of power and influence involved, and allegiance to party is a means by which seats on Congressional committees are maintained, but such factors alone are not sufficient to explain allegiance to party despite policy disagreement marking large blocs of Southern voters.

Allegiance to party that persists in disregard of policy position, especially when another party more adequately represents goals in which a person believes, is a form of idolatry. It puts party allegiance above convictions concerning what is right and just. It may even take its measure of what is right and just from the changes in the party line that occur either with rapid reversals or slow evolution. This behavior is so obvious in the case of the Communist that we have learned to suspect and scorn it—but it is by no means clear that the Communists have a monopoly on party idolatry of this type. They make the process extreme, and undergo flips of attitude in quick obedience to orders from above, but they are not the only men who have professed loyalty to a party "be it right or wrong."

We are not complaining at this point about the person

who remains loyal to a party despite temporary and minor differences he has with its current policies. There is a place in politics, as in all forms of human life, for exercising compromise and observing the art of the possible. Loyalty to party may mean continual efforts to effect changes of policy from within, to seek for goals that differ in many ways from those presently implemented, to accept decisions that one personally does not favor. But loyalty to party must not result in an uncritical allegiance that seems unable to work for changes of party loyalty, unable to take issue with positions put forth at a given time by the controlling group.

The idolatry of party allegiance is most dangerous in the person who is least directly involved in party struggle. The person who votes blindly for the Republican or Democratic candidate because he has done so continuously for the past ten, twenty, or even forty years, is caught placing uncritical devotion in a human structure. Politicians can count on the unquestioning support of such a person, and they go their merry way in blissful disregard of whatever notions such a voter may entertain about the role of government in human affairs. While political independence is preferable to this kind of party idolatry, it may not be as valuable as active participation in the policy decisions of the organization itself.

It is a parlor sport of long standing to be condescending toward politicians who change their attitudes in response to the shifting of political winds. Opposing candidates in the primary will patch up their differences before the main election. Bitter as contestants in intraparty feuds, they are "friends" and co-workers when their party is running against the other side. And what is thus true of intraparty struggle may also be true of contests between the parties. Campaign oratory is meant in earnest, but not too much; the loser will congratulate the winner without insisting that all his dire predictions surely will come true.

But the parlor sport neglects an important truth. Unless political process can be taken with enough grains of salt to make such reversals of attitude viable, a democratic process is not possible. When politics is "played for keeps" and fences are not mended, ranks not closed behind the winner, and the hostilities of opposing parties not allowed to burn out harmlessly, we are in a situation of tension, revolution, and uncertainty. Revolutionaries struggle with political power with no willingness to accept defeat in a fair contest, and because their loyalty to their cause is made absolute, their presence in the social unit is dangerous. Any political struggle "played for keeps" is more bitter than one played with the possibilities of changing one's mind, reversing one's smaller loyalties, and taking back one's oratory. The vicissitudes and seeming mockeries of political gamesmanship may have more health than the bitter hostilities of contests undertaken from unbending conviction. The opposing parties in the desegregation battles that whirl about the effort to integrate schools in the South and housing in the North struggle against each other with such deep conviction that the battle will leave scars.

It is a seeming paradox that idolatry appears in those who do not take political struggle seriously enough to know what is at stake as well as those who take it so seriously as to make it absolute. The person of traditional party allegiance is like the person of blind religious faith —he is strongly loyal for unknown and inadequately understood reasons. He may be insecure and cover his insecurity with dogmatic and unquestioning zeal. The person whose participation in political conflict is motivated so deeply from intense concern that he cannot bounce with political fortune and ride the bandwagon when necessary may be like an entrenched priest—he has so deep a loyalty that he makes it brittle and unbending. Unbending loyalty is as rigid in its behavior as unquestioning faith is unthinking in its understanding of truth. In either, the loyalty structure is idolatrous and the consequence grave.

The kind of commitment to a group that persists irrespective of the policies advocated by the group and just illustrated by the conventional Old Guard of a political party is also evident in a certain kind of allegiance to the nation. The phrase "my country right or wrong" has been both voiced and followed by the majority of citizens in the modern nation-state. Reversals of national intention and policy are accepted by most citizens as a matter of course, and the judgment as to what is right is made with reference to who performs an act or pursues a policy rather than by reference to what policy is pursued.

Blind and fervent allegiance to nation becomes jingoism in the context of struggle. Not only does the jingo glorify the exploits of war as a channel of glory, and portray his cause as a righteous crusade, but he gives a total loyalty to his nation-state. Every possibility of scrutiny and judgment over the actions of his nation is aborted by the intensity of his devotion and the one-sidedness of his perspective. This effect is most apparent when struggle is involved and the passions generated by the process of struggle are more idolatrous than are the normal degrees of concern for the welfare of one's homeland.

Not all love of country is idolatrous. Indeed, the love of country in many nations is related to the service of many more transcendent human goals, and even in time of war countries may undertake to defend values that are important to other nations and other peoples. The passions of war, however, breed intense loyalties that make involvement with struggle veer toward the furious. Unless such involvement is kept under scrutiny and judgment, idolatry is a continual danger.

Some chaplains in World War II found themselves in difficulty at precisely the point at which they sought to exercise such scrutiny. Prompted by the theological understanding current in many sophisticated circles at the time, they preached the judgment of God against both sides in the conflict. They spoke of the sin within the fabric of the Allied nations as well as the gross evil in the social systems against which the allies fought. The commanders, not versed in the subtleties of Niebuhrian thought, frequently were annoyed by the seeming equivocation and even disturbed at what they saw as a diluted loyalty to the war effort. The chaplains were men of no less devotion to the cause they served than were the commanders, but they could acknowledge the evil aspects of their own position whereas the commanders could only make a black and white distinction between opposing sides.

The tension of struggle may actually tempt men to regard their cause as more righteous than it truly is. No human cause is fully righteous, and many human causes mix righteous and ignoble elements. When the proximate righteousness of a relatively good cause is set in juxtaposition to the obvious malignancy of a socially destructive cause, it is easy to think in terms of black and white instead of in terms of differing shades of gray. Every battle in human history is a seedbed for the oversimplification of issues, and it takes a prophet sent from God to see that the righteousness of the righteous nation is infected with evil as well as the malignancy that has conquered the "evil" one.

Those who participate in war by simple acquiescence to what they are told to do are in greatest danger of having their conduct determined by a false allegiance. To ask no questions about the enterprise, to submit without question to the draft, to the rigors of military training, and to fight with implicit confidence in the righteousness of one's own nation is to abandon the moral duty of man. To let the agencies of patriotic fervor hold full and unchallenged sway over one's thinking is to sell the soul to a false god. Many agencies find in the symbolism and enthusiasm of coercive struggle the greatest and most powerful basis for their appeal. This problem grows in proportion to the extent to which war takes on the features of the crusade. The parade is more than an appeal to the senses; it can be a ritual to a false god.

Those who have encountered convinced and vocal pacifists in debate will realize that their position is not immune from idolatry and one-sidedness. Some pacifists spend their time attacking all military leaders as either misguided or deliberately malicious, and one gets the impression from hearing them speak that the Pentagon is the root of all evil. In other instances they have tried to offset prevailing attitudes about an enemy by trying to whitewash the motives and deeds of the opposing nation. Both procedures are understandable in the heat of conflict and debate, but they can develop into twisted judgments and warped views. The tendency of struggle to make men think in terms of black and white appears in this case as a blanket condemnation of all those who are not pacifists.

It is common to regard confessions of one's own shortcomings as a sign of weakness. In conflict, weakness is an invitation to defeat. But there is a weakness born of pride rather than of humility. The proud rabbit proverbially loses the race to the plodding turtle. Certainly pride infects all men, especially in the processes of conflict. This pride is manifest in the esthetic glorification of combat and struggle, in the moral pretensions of the crusade, and in the idolatry of cause by which the self regards its actions as the enactments of holiness itself. Men seldom become as pretentious in conditions of peace and security as they do in situations of struggle and conflict.

Esthetic dislike of struggle is an inadequate basis with which to judge it, and men who react to their likes or dislikes betray their responsible obligations. Moral objection to struggle is a sounder and more valid witness to problems involved in resort to violence and conflict, but in itself it does not dispose of all the issues struggle poses. The theological analysis of struggle as a matter of human loyalties and their possible misdirection focuses attention upon the way in which struggle is embraced. It opens the possibility that the manner in which men conduct a struggle may have more bearing upon their spiritual situation and their behavior than whether or not they conduct it at all. A sensitive, sore-pressed, and soul-searching participation in struggle may be more valid and profound from the standpoint of religious faith than self-righteous jingoism or self-righteous objection. If withdrawal from struggle is to make sense, it must also be soul-searching, sore-pressed, and aware of the limited achievement of all human responses to the exigencies of life.

The fundamental task of the prophetic religious voice in a situation of struggle is to insist upon those reactions to all forms of conflict that bring them under the judgment of God. Merely to urge that men enter struggle as the channel of involvement in the stuff of history is to give religious sanctions to their normal inclinations. On the other hand, to urge men to stand aside because of devotion to some transcendent absolute is to make religion an escape from life. We must learn to understand struggle, bring it under scrutiny and judgment, use it or reject it in response to our understanding of God's will in given circumstances, and employ and reject it only with a sense of the inadequacy of all human achievements. To do this requires that struggle be understood, not as something good or bad in its own right, but as an instrument related to the loyalties that capture the allegiance of men.

IV

THE INSECURITY OF THE SELF AND THE DESTRUCTION OF THE OTHER: THE ANATOMY OF STRUGGLE

ALMOST all forms of struggle are undertaken in the effort to secure the self from threats of discomfort or extinction or else in the effort to preserve some value that is cherished by the self. This affects both the techniques and the motives of struggle, and has consequences for all moral arguments about its legitimacy. The diverse forms of struggle are alike in the fact that all of them are related to the effort to secure the self. Many of the spiritual problems surrounding struggle are connected with this attempt.

Street-corner debates and dormitory bull sessions have endlessly underscored the right of self-defense as the most compelling sanction for armed conflict. Self-defense is the effort to save the self from privation or extinction, and has long been commonly regarded as both the justification for conflict and one of its prime results. Few nations have undertaken military operations except as prompted to seek their security in a world of threat and change. The role of national self-interest plays a large place in the deliberations of diplomats, generals, and ordinary citizens. Some carefree and blithe individuals join the Navy "to see the world," but the fundamental motive of most men for taking up arms is to protect themselves in a world where security seems purchased by power.

It is frequently pointed out that citizen soldiers make better fighters than mercenary troops. The citizen fights for the defense of house and family, and for the security of a self that yearns for the fruits of victory and the return to home. The footloose mercenary has no deep concern either about the outcome of a battle or the speed of victory. A loyalty "sold" to one commander can be bartered to another, and the man without a country is not likely to care which one succeeds. Professional soldiers, on the other hand, even though they also fight for money, are bound to a particular nation and are more highly motivated than mercenaries. They possess zeal and conviction born of identity with the interests of their nation-states and not from soldiering as a means of monetary gain.

But while self-defense may be the most commonly acknowledged motive for coercive struggle it is not the most justified one. Self-defense in the narrow sense is an appeal to motives that can be charged as selfish. The defense of a cherished value is a somewhat higher motive for coercive struggle. The obligation to protect an innocent child from the attack of a bully or a senior lady from the rampages of a madman seems almost self-evident. A man may deny the importance of defending himself against attack but it is less easy to deny the importance of defending someone else. Those who refuse their duty to defend others have been scorned as weaklings, attacked as traitors, or placed in cells and detention camps.

Insofar as both presuppose the use of force and violence, the interventionist is morally superior to the political isolationist, since the interventionist accepts the duty to defend a neighbor who is in danger rather than waiting to employ arms until he himself is attacked. In calling for the repeal of the Neutrality Act of 1939, Reinhold Niebuhr declared it "one of the most immoral laws that was ever spread upon a federal statute book," and observed:

When a great fire has broken out in a small town, responsible citizens who are in a position to do something about it do not draw their shutters, lock their doors, and crawl under their beds. To do so would be to forfeit forever moral authority in their community. The Christian ethic requires these citizens to go out on the street and do whatever may be necessary to help their fellows bring the fire under control. (*Christianity and Crisis,* October 20, 1941, pp. 1 f. Used by permission.)

Political isolationism rests in large measure upon the premise that while self-defense is legitimate, it should be employed only when an attack has been made upon home territory. To be sure, some intervention has been advocated from equally selfish motives—to keep the fighting overseas and away from home territory, but this is not an inherent feature of the position. Intercontinental ballistics will do much to nullify any future use of such a selfish pragmatism; to intervene in any future world crisis will be to invite destruction of home base as well as the territory of the "helped" neighbor.

Paul Ramsey bluntly states: *"Self-defense is the worst of all possible excuses for war or for any other form of resistance."* (*Basic Christian Ethics,* p. 173. Charles Scribner's Sons, 1950. Italics his.) The defense of a needy neighbor is probably the best excuse for resort to arms. In between we find the violence undertaken to defend a cherished value. When such a value is important to the self alone its defense is less justified than when it is important to other men as well. Shrewd statesmen know better than to resort to violence without portraying it as a means of preserving some important cultural or political value. It is not mere cynicism that cloaks military enterprise with moral rationalizations of this sort, but a tacit realization that the defense of a cherished value has a profounder moral justification than the defense of the self.

Struggles undertaken in defense of a cherished value are not any less violent than those pursued in self-defense. Indeed, they may even be more bitter. When man's loyalties are attached to noble causes, or causes that he deems noble, he is capable of greater sacrifice than he will exhibit in defense of his own skin. Religious wars, for example, are often bitter wars because the commitments of religion are more deeply seated than those of almost any other human loyalties. Revolutionary movements convinced of their duty to "liberate" the masses exhibit extreme harshness, sparing no means to secure their ends, and evidencing few qualms in the liquidation of their foes.

The attempt to secure the corporate self is obvious in the case of resistance to armed attack, but the posture of aggression is often as much an expression of the effort to secure the self as is the posture of defense. In a world of change, security for some is enhanced by inciting change and magnifying the uncertainties of international relationships. Only the powerful and successful profit from letting the *status quo* persist indefinitely, and the disinherited and insecure may prompt trouble from the very same effort to secure the self that leads the prosperous to keep it down.

Struggle emerges from the effort of the self to obtain security, but the realities of struggle frequently undercut the securities of those who resort to its use. As a means of gaining security for the self much struggle is self-defeating because it sets men at variance with other men who are also seeking to secure themselves. Ironically, the limited value of struggle does not seem to deter men from resorting to it as a means of attempting to secure the self. There is pathos and irony in any arms race. The possession and multiplication of arms breeds greater distrust and higher tensions between the participants at the very same time the participants are building arms in the effort to secure their corporate selves against aggression. This pathos is not removed by moral exhortation or overcome by high idealism, and the results of seeking to remove it unilaterally are almost never happy. Thus begins a vicious circle in which everyone feels compelled to do what he prefers not to do, and finds that what he does confounds his aims rather than confirms his hopes. Few patterns in corporate social life show the human plight in starker terms than an arms race wanted by neither contender yet trusted by both.

Acts of heroism express much the same irony. In the effort to defend a cherished value the hero may sacrifice himself and be cut off from the value. The man who lays down his life for his friend demonstrates the greatest form of love, but he also robs his companion of a desired associate. The man whose life is spared by the heroic sacrifice of another does not rejoice. He appreciates the tragic dimensions of life that are frequently the channels of its highest values.

While heroism can be an expression of the highest form of love, it can also be turned into a means by which to secure the self. Cold calculation of consequence may lead men to perform the heroic act as a means of self-aggrandizement. In perhaps the most powerful of all the powerful scenes in T. S. Eliot's *Murder in the Cathedral*, Thomas à Becket wrestles with the temptation to engineer his martyrdom in order to secure his reputation as a saint. He concludes that "martyrdom is never the design of man," but this conclusion is not so clearly recognized in all cases. Saint Ignatius felt his martyrdom coming, but did not perceive its implications with the help of a playwright, as did Becket. Hence, he wrote to the church at Rome:

Grant me nothing more than to be poured out in sacrifice to God, while there is still an altar ready, so that you may form a chorus in love and sing to the Father through Jesus Christ, because God has deemed the bishop of Syria worthy to be found at the setting of the sun, summoning him from the sunrise. It is good to set from the world unto God, so that I may rise with him. (Edgar J. Goodspeed, *The Apostolic Fathers: An American Translation,* pp. 221 f. Harper & Brothers, 1950. Used by permission.)

The honor given to the hero is often earned, but if sought for its benefit to self, may represent a subtle yet powerful temptation to pride. To suggest that even the martyr is not immune from possible self-interest is not to rule out the legitimacy of martyrdom, but to recognize that it may become an instrument of struggle. Martyrdom may be infused with the sin of human pride as completely as cowardice is infused with the sin of human disloyalty. Under such conditions it spoils its own grandeur.

The relationship between the security of the self and resort to coercive violence is obvious. In what sense does nonviolent coercion raise the same problem? The goals of independence and equality that have been sought through the use of nonviolent action represent a type of security for their seekers, an enhancement of the self, a value that can and should be cherished by all men. Groups that have used this kind of technique have been seeking something for themselves and for others that in other constellations of power they might obtain by violence. They struggle because of the need for a status for the self—in the case of the bus boycotts and lunch-counter sit-ins an elementary human dignity and the right to ride on the same basis as other passengers or be served alongside of other men. We dare not deny to men the right to struggle for such dignity and security, even though we must analyze it as an effort alloyed with self-interest.

Self-interest is present in conquest as well as in coercion, though it takes different forms. Conquests of the unknown serve to make the self more secure, not only when the unknown can be brought under dominion and controlled for human betterment, but even when it is possible merely

knowledge are steps to the control of nature, and eventually even of man, but forget that a rise in potential is subject to both good and evil applications.

To accept the fact that new problems plague new achievements is not to deny the value of the achievements or to argue for the rejection of the struggle to conquer the unknown. Those who feel the need to set a moratorium on human exploration may have diagnosed the problem more profoundly than those who have easy and optimistic hopes for what will come of future conquest. But they make a false prescription because they believe the ambiguities that attend conquest can be overcome by stopping the process itself. Conquest involves risk, and frequently a greater rather than a lesser degree of security for the self. Its rejection, however, involves stagnation and a false kind of security that proves unsatisfactory. To wish, for example, that knowledge of atomic fission be explored no further because bombs might be made more terrible is to look for security where it does not lie and to settle for the precarious situation of the present. To assume that further development of knowledge in these fields will lessen the insecurities that are presently involved is to misread the normal consequences of events. The security of the self cannot be assured by any level of technical mastery over nature. To hope for security from this source is either to create an insatiable yet unquenchable demand for greater effort or else to reject the whole process itself, killing its creative as well as its threatening fruits.

The insecurity that attends the fruits of discovery is further evidenced in the extent to which nations go to guard and protect what they have discovered, lest other nations obtain the secret. In the effort to secure themselves against each other, nations race in the conquest of nature. The race breeds insecurity and thus further compounds its own necessity. A successful orbital flight around the world by one of the major powers compounds envy with fear in the others. Each nation wants the prestige that will come from being first to land a man on the moon. There is bitter irony in this process. Science, extolled by many philosophers as the most public form of truth is often guarded by elaborate security precautions designed to keep it secret to a given nation-state. Even the conquest of nature has become an occasion for competition.

The intimate relationship between competitive struggle and the effort to secure the self needs little elaboration here. In an era when novelists and playwrights examine the gray-flannel suit and the status scramble of suburbia no alert observer will question the connection between competitive struggle and the effort to obtain status security for the self. The devices by which the self seeks through competition to secure its status or to enhance its standing are as myriad as the forms of competitive struggle itself. The competitive dimensions in every human situation, from kindergarten to old-age colony, are potentially present and frequently stark.

In competitive struggle two primary means of seeking self-aggrandizement are the ownership of goods and demonstration of superior competence. Suburban living has put a premium on the former; the academic world frequently puts a premium on the latter. When the teacher says to Johnny, "You're not keeping up with the class," the appeal is to Johnny's desire to secure his self in relation to others. Similar motives are played upon by the goading salesman of a home improvement company, who, wishing to clinch a sale, says to Mrs. Jones, "Your neighbor has just put a new porch on his house. Don't you think your house needs a new porch?" Anyone familiar with the machinations of any large social group in which men scramble for position knows how closely the element of competition can become related to the effort to secure the self against threat and change.

Adaptability is an ironical way to engage in competitive struggle. The person who conforms to the group may compete with other members of the group, not by overt scramble, but by subtle efforts to secure and advance himself. The art of apple-polishing is a long-practiced subterfuge for competing with others without stamping on them. It curries the favor of the ruling masters, frequently by becoming subservient to their desires. It is easier done when the masters are few in number and stay in power for long periods of time than it is done in situations where authority lines are fluid. Apple-polishing is less successful in a democracy or an oligarchy than it is in a benevolent tyranny because it is more difficult to get on the favorable side of a shifting or complex authority than to become the favorite of a single boss.

Efforts to secure the self competitively, either by winning a contest for status or by finding favor in the eyes of the powers that be, are seldom decisive and often self-defeating. The climber can never be sure that he will stay on top or continue to find favor in the eyes of superiors. By setting selves against one another competition breeds a distrust that destroys the very sense of security it seeks. Not everyone can win a contest; most men have to lose. The danger of losing becomes a greater threat following each success, because men of high status have the most to lose from a reversal of fortune. A self that seeks security through submission to peers and elders erodes its own independence and thwarts its own attempts to become secure.

The failure of our technically proficient and materially comfortable civilization to furnish real security for the self is manifest. The enlarging population of mental hospitals despite significant increases in the percentage of cures and the growing instances of psychosomatic medical difficulties appearing in doctors' offices are bred in part from the emotional tensions of a status-seeking age, and mainly from the competitive types of struggle that have come to dominate it. That the struggle is more subtle than ruthless and more covert than acknowledged appears only to magnify the problem rather than to meliorate it.

In the struggle to secure the self by coercion, conquest, or competition the security of the self is attained by the attempted destruction of an opposing self. The intended destruction may take differing forms—from mere confinement or neutralization to actual elimination. Some of these ways of destroying others are worse than other ways, and discriminating judgments between them are both possible and necessary. Even so, the effort to secure oneself at the expense of another is a feature of struggle in all its types.

War heightens this tension to the ultimate degree. "Kill or be killed!" An enemy in war is brought to submission by threatened extinction. The threat may not be carried out, and even in armed conflict there are mitigating circumstances that keep the ultimate sanction from being used too often. One such factor is willingness to make prisoners of those who surrender. Roger Shinn tells a story of a front line encounter in which the pressures of conflict made even this impossible.

It was in one of the heavy forests of western Germany. The infantry company had advanced through the woods the day before, cleaning out the enemy groups that lingered there. Casualties had been heavy, and the company would be under strength for today's action. Yesterday, a few Germans had pretended to surrender, and then had fired, costing the Americans several lives. This morning the company would continue the same slow, weary advance.

A sergeant had been commanding one of the platoons, since the officer had been killed. He got the orders for the day's movement. There was a new element in the orders today. "Take no prisoners." The company, now under strength, could not afford more casualties to the enemy's trickery. Even if they succeeded in capturing Germans, they could no longer spare the men to escort the prisoners to the rear. (*Beyond This Darkness*, by Roger Shinn, pp. 51 f. Association Press, 1946. Used by permission.)

War prisoners are presumably neutralized as opponents —though codes of conduct call for them to make every effort to escape confinement and carry on the struggle. The effectiveness of an opponent for military purposes is destroyed when he is imprisoned. Brainwashing of prisoners seeks to carry the process of neutralization one more step—to destroy the selfhood of the prisoner by leaving him without passion for escape or the desire to return to his original set of loyalties. It represents a departure from those few "rules of the game" that are still accepted in total war.

Total war raises grave issues regarding the moral consequences of all coercive techniques and makes the appeal to self-defense anachronistic. To say that one will not strike back unless first hit by an aggressor is to invite a blow that in the condition of modern nuclear warfare may be fatal. To wait for the first blow to be struck by the other side is to invite disaster if the other side strikes at all. Willingness to destroy the opponent is presupposed in any effective system of coercion, and under modern conditions even the willingness to strike first at reasonable provocation may need to be conceded by those whose main basis of judgment is military necessity. It is therefore impossible to consider the moral implications of coercive struggle without acknowledging the fundamental thrust to destroy the opponent. This thrust is less easy to justify than the effort to secure the self.

Similarly, total war carries the destruction of the opponent to the ultimate limit represented by brainwashing. Where, from the standpoint of a fight to the absolute finish, is the rationale for rejecting the use of this "weapon" as a means of neutralizing or destroying opponents? It is not enough to decry the technique because it was used by others to our disadvantage. We must have some moral grounds of decision that declare it wrong in substance and not merely in consequences.

The destruction of the opponent in competition is less ruthless than in coercion and is present to the extent that the rules governing fair play cease to operate effectively. Under rules men seek to win—to secure themselves or enhance their status—but without rules men seek to tear down the opposition by every means at their command that they can get away with. All the terms that are used to describe bitter competition imply destruction of the opponent: cutthroat, knock-down-and-drag-out, to the bitter end.

The politics of revolutionary situations show that political life may contain the effort to destroy the opponent. Firing squads, concentration camps, and kangaroo courts multiply in situations where the rules of political fair play are absent or forgotten. They move political struggle from the clearly competitive to the nearly coercive level and blur any intended line of sharp demarcation between them.

Milder efforts to destroy an opponent appear in the political life of established and stable societies. One of the effective techniques employed is the smear, in which an opponent's reputation and good standing are undercut in order to reduce his influence. The smear has a long and sordid history and a multitude of expressions. Witch-hunts are built upon its use. Guilt by association pays political dividends when the public cannot discount the bad logic upon which it builds a case. Name-calling of any sort is a form of smearing, especially where the names have heavy emotive connotations. To call a political party "lovers of big business" is less of a smear than to call it "a band of traitors," but illustrates the same technique.

The sneer is a milder form of smear, but it also is an

effort to destroy an opponent and its uses are legion in the annals of political controversy. The sneer would destroy, not by outright verbal bombast, but by a mixture of irony and humor concocted to discredit the reputation or image of its victim. A study of the sneer in contemporary politics could make both sordid and amusing reading, and logical analysis of the slogans employed in controversy would suggest that emotive language is far more common than cognitive claims. Indeed, to ignore emotive language is to overlook the kind of discourse that runs the world.

One of the values in formal debate is that one learns to expose and turn back upon the aggressor the use of smear and sneer. But formal debate is a discipline of the few, and its amenities have long since evaporated from the arena of public discussion of political affairs. The salesman approach encroaches, Madison Avenue runs the campaigns, and the multiplication of negative emotive symbols in use against opponents bids fair to swamp the kind of arguments over issues upon which intelligent decision rests.

For that matter even the issues are cast into emotive terms. The difference between the two major parties is described as a difference in their attitude toward "big government." "Big government" is an emotive term. It describes a certain trend, but its vagueness permits the hearer to create his own connotations. By fastening the label "big government" or "big business" upon opponents one can set in motion the kind of public reactions that will destroy his chances of victory, while at the same time avoiding distinct commitments about specific issues or sharp delineations of one's own policy decisions. This creates struggle by trickery.

One needs only to look at the great controversies of our time to see how fully they are fought with smears and sneers, not only in political life but in economic and community affairs as well. The discussions of medical economics seldom commend themselves as model illustrations of rational argument; the attacks upon the Supreme Court following its decision on public school desegregation have not exhibited polite restraint or cogent grasp of the moral implications of constitutional procedures; right-to-work legislation is cleverly and deceptively named; and any community that confronts the moral question of open occupancy in housing for all groups of citizens will surely be engulfed in a barrage of emotive slogans.

Since competition is marked by techniques that seek to run down others as well as to secure the self, it is never a fully satisfactory channel for the development of confidence or sense of ease. Even the winners cannot be sure they will remain on top, and the precariousness of position is a direct function of its degree of attainment. The dictum of Karl Marx that the workers of the world have "nothing to lose but their chains" proves untrue when the same workers become rulers and employ chains in the effort to keep other workers from revolting against their lordship. Power corrupts, for it represents a victory from competition that because of its insecurity must reduce the free competition that strives against it. Victors in competition may resort to coercion to entrench their gains unless there is a wider context of accepted standards within which they find enough security as selves.

In his play, *The Sign of Jonah,* Guenter Rutenborn analyzes the problem of the ruler. Writing from the experiences of his nation during its Nazi rule, he finds a parallel in the story of the Queen of Sheba. One by one the characters of the play come forth to justify their part in the construction of the fiery furnaces that swallowed up the people of God. Their excuses basically plead the necessity of preserving life for themselves or their loved ones by consenting to the debauchery and terror. The Queen herself pleads the necessity of keeping order by destroying those who threaten it. Before the bar of justice, crushed and resentful, the Queen states her case and in bitter resentment cries out against the Creator of a world in which such action seems necessary to maintain order.

Yes, I ordered the furnaces built! It had to be! I was compelled to do it! My position demands that I lead my people, give them laws to preserve order among them, for man left to himself is chaos. In order to enforce the laws I had to be severe. I was forced to kill in order to preserve life. Who created man in such fashion that only the threat of death and terror make him manageable? God! Who arranged the world in such fashion that kings must commit greater sins than other mortals? God! Who forces us to keep our nations alive by leading them up to the altar of war, to be bled white? God! (From *The Sign of Jonah*. Copyrighted by Guenter Rutenborn and George White, 1960, and published by Thomas Nelson & Sons, New York. Used by permission.)

Resentment against God is the final form of the intended destruction of the Other. It may affect not only the rulers of men and the architects of coercion but those who struggle against the elements. God is resented because he stands in judgment over the necessities of struggle and qualifies man's right to conduct it in any manner he sees fit.

Conquest of nature would seem at first thought to be free from the possibility of an intended destruction of the Other. Few scientists are driven by the intention to usurp power for their personal selves from the conquest of nature, but they may contribute to a corporate effort to conquer nature with such thoroughness as to remove all contingencies. They may forget their personal responsibility for both conducting and portraying their enterprise as shared co-operation with a Creator whose power stands over all human achievement and thus give comfort to the secularization of the conquest of nature. Daniel Day Williams has observed the subtle yet very crucial consequences that follow when nature is used without reverence.

When man regards nature only as something to be exploited for immediate gain without concern for the whole good it is meant to serve, he loses even his capacity to make full use of nature. A scientific conquest of nature without the sense of reverence will always turn against us. Mind becomes calculating, practical, sure of its capacity to dominate. Yet this imperial confidence of man the exploiter has nothing to serve. It loses the zest of life. It has no power to see it whole. That is much of what is wrong with man's spirit today. Sheer control over life for the sake of control is self-defeating. The good earth is good only as we love it in the using of it. (*God's Grace and Man's Hope,* p. 164. Harper & Brothers, 1949. Used by permission.)

Struggle is secularized when it is conducted without reference to God and his possible judgments over it. The thrust to absolute mastery of nature or of man as a child of nature represents the secularization of conquest; the brutal politics of totalitarianism represents the secularization of competitive struggle; total war represents the secularization of coercive struggle. In each case the security of the self is sought through its own mastery of conflicting vitalities and the conflicting vitalities are mastered by their threatened destruction.

V

THE DEFENDER AND THE REVOLUTIONARY: STRUGGLE AND SOCIAL CHANGE

POLITICAL and social institutions are frequently changed by a process of struggle. Sometimes the struggle takes place within a framework of accepted patterns that makes possible smooth transition and orderly movement from one established order to another. More frequently the struggle takes a violent and revolutionary form. Americans with a sense of history will appreciate the relationship of struggle to social change. Born in a revolution, torn asunder by an internal war in middle youth, presently racked by struggles for equality and justice at home, and tensed by the task of preserving freedom in the world, our nation is no stranger to the reality of social change and the struggle that accompanies it. The national anthem does not sing about a peaceful Nirvana, even though our unconscious self-image may be dominated by an illusion that we never hurt anyone. Nor do we desire to stagnate in our plenty even though some small groups might wish us to return to a state in which our riches were less evenly divided.

Regardless of whether social change occurs within an enduring political order or by the overflow of one order for another, some men oppose social change and others seek it. Each may be convinced that he acts for mankind's benefit or for the common good of his immediate community, cloaking his actions with appropriate justifications and sanctions. But despite the similarities, individual men and social groups behave differently as the defenders of an existing order than as revolutionaries against it. The roles of defender and revolutionary challenge men in different ways and create peculiar temptations that are associated with each role. Not all men behave the same way in the same role, but general observations are not impossible. The individual who would defend an existing order, either from inertia or conviction, should understand the temptations and dangers of such defense; the individual who would challenge a present state of affairs, either from discontent or the thrust for new justice, must likewise know what he is about.

Every existing social order is sufficiently just to be viewed as a preserver of some order and value—at least by its defenders. When a self becomes identified with the values preserved by a present state of affairs, however limited in range or virtue such values may be, it identifies its own security with the perpetuation of the *status quo.* This identity can be expressed in many ways, most of which involve generically religious types of commitment. The specifically religious forms of such identity sanctify a particular order as the creation of God and seek its preservation as a divinely ordained instrument for maintaining goodness and restraining evil in the body politic. Pseudo-religious forms of the identity of the self with an existing order attribute an inordinate importance to the present state of affairs and remove it from scrutiny and criticism. In the first instance, change is resisted because opposition to the powers in control is considered tantamount to rebellion against the Creator; in the second instance, change is resisted because disloyalty to the existing order is conceived as treason. Both rebellion against God and treason against the state are purged by the defenders of a *status quo* because they threaten the structure of security to which they cling. The phenomenon is no less real in a hunt for subversives than in the operation of an Inquisition—though the form it takes and the victims it makes are different in each case.

On the other hand, every existing social order may be accused of perpetuating injustices and entrenching existing evils. Criticism of such orders is often as plausible as their defense, and there are hardly any social systems that cannot be found wanting in at least some feature of their order. The victim of social oppression or the person whose destiny has been ill-treated by the existing state of affairs may frequently feel that his destiny is tied up with its modification if not with its destruction. The zeal of the reformer and the fanaticism of the rebel are born in part from the effort to overplay the inadequacies of an existing order in order to justify its modification. The judgment justly made against certain aspects of the *status quo* is universalized into a condemnation of the whole. Conversely, the defenders of the *status quo* seek the entrenchment of the whole to preserve its partial values.

It is not difficult to gather academic and detached assent to the proposition that all human accomplishments are limited and partial. In moments of unruffled reflection, men will generally concede that there are no perfect social orders. But in the process of struggle these insights are eclipsed by the overwhelming impulse to see an existing order as a total good that must be preserved or as a total evil that must be destroyed. We acknowledge relative justice and partial accomplishments in reflective moments, but in the heat of battle we forget how relative and partial they are. The defender thus overplays the values of the *status quo,* while the adversary challenges the whole edifice and not merely the specific wrongs within it.

This is true, not only in revolutionary upheavals where

the tension between the defender and the adversary is drawn to fever pitch, but in many minor contests that take place in political affairs. The adversary sees the defender as a scoundrel, corrupted by his enjoyment of existing power, fruitless in his exercise of office, and fit only for defeat and removal. The cry to "throw the rascals out" is based upon the oversimplification of issues. It exaggerates criticism of incumbents, it implies a drastic need of cure when minor medication might suffice, and it presupposes that new incumbents will not become rascals in their own way. The defender, on the other hand, sees the adversary as a threat, driven by the desire to snatch power and to overturn the values of the present regime. Thus he oversimplifies the issues by urging people "not to trust the ship of state to inexperienced radicals" and seeks to undermine the confidence of the electorate in the wisdom and integrity of the challenger.

The defender of the *status quo* is at both a moral and strategic disadvantage in this contest even though he holds the advantages of power and position. He is at a moral disadvantage because it is worse to whitewash the partially corrupt than it is to criticize the relatively good. The inner moral thrust of prophetic faith is always a judgment more impressed with the evil inherent in existing orders than with the values served by preserving them. The priestly temperament may turn the matter around and be more concerned about the possible loss of a value than excited by the gain of a good. It may even seek to stifle the prophetic word or render it ineffective by pointing out the overdrawn criticism. The prophetic hero speaks forth with a radical thrust that sets all human partialities against more ultimate standards of achievement and truth. The defender of an existing order bases his case upon gratitude for the relative accomplishments at hand. The priest seems less heroic and upright than the prophet because his contentment with the partial is less appealing than a high vision of the absolute.

The strategic disadvantage of the defender stems from his identity with the existing order. The critic can make judgments without proposing alternatives or bearing responsibilities for results, but the defender of the present order must limit his actions to responsible moves and must defend the actions even when they are far from perfect. He becomes the object of hatred and scorn when the actions that he takes restrict the license of some in favor of the wider good of many. The ambiguity of human accomplishment plagues his path by mixing with every step he takes to achieve a degree of tolerable justice those elements of dissatisfaction that are inherent in the fabric of every social structure. It is easy for the contender to criticize the "powers that be," particularly if he bears no responsibility for implementing alternative means for accomplishing the ends he advocates. To the extent that college faculty members are denied or tend to shun responsibility for administrative affairs they find great sport in sniping at the "head office." The same is true in the business organization, the structured church, or any unit of the Armed Forces. In politics the opposition party is sure that the present administration is headed by duped dopes, and the private citizen takes great glee in criticizing the operation of "the government" unless the glee is denied to him by totalitarian edict. Moreover, the glee is more obvious in the case of "armed chair" observers than in the case of those who are responsibly active in politic affairs.

There is no ruler or leader with sufficient skill to please all men. Indeed, rulers who seek to please all men are frequently weak and ineffective, bringing disgrace to their office and criticism to themselves. It is impossible to remove all criticism, and the person in power must be prepared to accept gibes as the price of leadership and authority. If he is not so prepared, he will either abdicate his position or seek to entrench it with methods that stifle any challenge.

Tyranny and dictatorship are sometimes born from the escalation of power that is created when a defender seeks to remove all threats to his rule. The defender will frequently exercise the prestige and the power of his office to stop criticism and to resist appeals for change. He may do this subtly by controlling channels of information and communication to create a better image of his rule than may be warranted; he may do it ruthlessly by coercive techniques designed to liquidate opposition. All kinds of rulers—political, ecclesiastical, academic, or economic— are guilty or at least open to this misuse of power. The danger is greatest when least recognized and most serious when the power of the ruler is exercised without the restraints of law or the check of contravailing power. Lord Acton placed his finger on the temptation inherent in rule when he observed that "all power corrupts," though his formulation of the maxim raises difficulties because it is unconditional. Moreover, absolute power and absolute corruption are imaginative abstractions rather than operational realities. Nevertheless, there are situations in which the defender of a *status quo* has been betrayed by an understandable effort to secure a stable order by thwarting opposition.

High ideals alone do not ward off this danger. The admonitions to humility found in much religion have not always kept religious leaders from wanton abuse of power. The slogans in favor of free enterprise do not ensure that business tycoons will preserve in practice the very competitive process to which they give lip service in theory. The ideals of the academic world concerning a sense of community among scholars and the value of open information freely sought are attained only in rare circumstances. Frequently it is those who pay the least verbal homage to freedom and openness who serve it with greatest devotion, and just relationships are sometimes more possible between groups in open conflict and tension than in situations dominated by entrenched power—regardless of its seeming benevolence.

When defenders of an existing order hold power strongly and use that power to their advantage in preserving their own privilege they create the conditions for radical revolution. The challenger resorts to techniques appropriate to the occasion, and when peaceful and persuasive methods are unsuccessful may resort to coercive and revolutionary tactics. Herbert Butterfield has suggested that many of the great struggles in international life since the First World War

> . . . have been caused by the fact that we have devised no satisfactory machinery for the peaceful revision of the *status quo*. The new machinery tended to freeze this more definitely than the old had been able to do. Treaties themselves may be unfair or unjust—or they may become so through the passage of time. But where the power which profits by the unjustice possesses a *liberum veto*, so that it can block any revision, there is great difficulty in securing a satisfactory arrangement. Because there has been a tendency to take refuge in legalism, it would seem that those who desire revision can always be made to appear as aggressors. (From *International Conflict in the Twentieth Century*, p. 31.)

This observation carefully avoids an uncritical identification of the challenger's case with the cause of righteousness and truth, but it does show the shadow of doubt that hangs over the defender's position. Both the defender and his adversary may be wrong though it is not likely that both will be right. Not every revolutionary thrust is justified or preferable to the perpetuation of the existing order, even when the existing order has outgrown its usefulness and lost its major virtues. "The Wave of the Future" may be backed by enthusiasm and express a just discontent with the present conditions around it, but this does not make it morally preferable by definition. Even when a revolutionary group is basically right in its criticism of an existing order its proposed substitution may not be warranted. The new order should replace the old only when it promises positive accomplishments as well as negative criticism.

The effort to bring about change often breeds resistance. Educational and persuasive processes can inch along in the attempted elimination of social evil, but an effective political move that sharply challenges the existing order may be met with bitter and even violent resistance. Many observers of the southern United States in the decade of the 1950's will testify that feelings ran higher following the school desegregation decision of the Supreme Court in 1954 than before the decision. Some will go so far as to wish nostalgically for the day when reason and persuasion seemed more evident than sit-ins, demonstrations, and the necessary use of troops at school yards. The radical challenge implicit in the decision and present in the efforts to implement it has created a reaction of intense proportions. Is it true, as some hold, that the progress made by persuasion and gradualism was more stable and even more likely to get an enduring result in a quicker time than direct challenge and assaults upon a social pattern?

There are no means by which controlled experiments can be conducted to settle this issue empirically, since there is no possibility of having a wide base of parallel situations to give the statistical foundation upon which scientific generalizations can be built. We deal with such a question within our view of history, and either find congenial the hope that gradual education and enlightenment can change social patterns or else are led to believe that the agonies of social struggle are the price paid for the achievement of justice. Our outlook is colored by our doctrine of man, our view of social process, our understanding of the role of self-interest in existing orders, and our esthetic reaction to struggle. Our outlook is also colored by our position in the struggle. Those who benefit from an existing state of affairs, even though they disapprove of it morally, may be more content to make progress slowly than those who are victims of the extant injustice. The defender can afford to be an idealist, to plead for gradual change, and to hope for orderly and calm transition when changes must be made. The challenger may deem the price paid for patience too high and demand a revolutionary readjustment that can be quickly achieved.

The hope for social change by slow and gradual process postulates no sharp and radical resistance to change on the part of man, because it has no probing doctrine of human sinfulness. It believes in persuasion rather than coercion, in moral influence rather than moral pressure, in change of heart rather than political shock. It does not take with sufficient seriousness the self-interest that deludes the defender of a *status quo* to imagine that his destiny is tied to the perpetuation of his present state. It supposes that the techniques of persuasion are gentle and easy to use, of good report and polite of execution. Cultures that have so read the human situation have poor records in the elimination of injustice and corruption though they often have a pleasant calm that those in privileged positions cherish and understandably enjoy.

There is little, if anything, in the Christian understanding of life to reinforce the assumption that gradual evolutionary processes constitute the normal patterns of human relations. Men whose self-interest is served by the maintenance of existing injustices are not persuaded by kindly words and high-sounding ideals to accept what they regard as the subjugation of the self-interest to the larger good. Only by the power of redemptive suffering are men shocked from their protection of self-interest to an acceptance of their responsibility in community on a purely voluntary basis.

Some years ago a group of idealistic citizens in a small community pressed for passage of an ordinance defining the minimal conditions of good housing and providing for the condemnation and elimination of substandard units. Many property owners opposed the law because they felt it to be an infringement of their right to control their own real estate, and even after the law was passed its enforcement was delayed. But then five children died in a fire that destroyed a shack which the housing code would have eliminated. The community was shocked into readiness to accept a law that might have languished for lack of support. The pretensions of the landlords to rights of property free from encroachments by the power of the state and opposition to the code based on the sacredness of ownership became less persuasive in the wake of a mass funeral than when advanced as high-sounding phrases in the normal course of political argument. Shock and pressure are frequently necessary to break the lethargy and complacency of a community that hesitates to act on a social problem or to eradicate some blight. The death of children is a high price for the assumption of social responsibility in a community—but history moves by the payment of high prices.

We are trained to respect and honor the willing sacrifice of the soldier but we have not learned to honor the heroic sacrifice of the social reformer. The challenger of the *status quo* must learn the costs and dangers of his role. He likely will be spurned and rejected by men who have no direct reason to oppose him as well as by those who are directly challenged by his actions. Most men belong to the *status quo* by default and inertia. Their religion is embalmed with it. They resent the challenger and wish both his cause and his person ill. The good solid citizens of a community prove so solid and thick that they tolerate the growth of injustice and abuse in order to avoid the unpleasantries of change. Efforts on behalf of change and reform therefore attract support from the disenfranchised and disinherited, the reckless and illiterate, more than from the stable and careful elements of a community. The consequence is a greater difficulty in effecting social change than might be the case if more socially prominent and economically stable people were found in causes of social reform. The blue blood who seeks the elimination of social caste and snobbery can certainly act more effectively and with more skill than the disinherited person from "the wrong side of the tracks." The financially successful businessman may have greater influence in bringing about economic justice than the person whose record in handling money leaves something to be desired.

A reformer who comes from the established order with credentials and pedigree may not only be a special asset to the cause of reform, but he is viewed with high suspicion from the ranks of those defending the *status quo*. The bitter, almost violent, hatred of elite social reformers by their social peers is the hatred of the elder son for the prodigal brother. No hatred is more vindictive. In the South today the aristocrat whose conscience leads him to active support of the thrust for racial justice is more bitterly hated than the outsider "who can't be expected to know any better." The traitor is more violently despised than the invader, and his role less frequently espoused.

Despite the risks, reformers do come from the houses of the privileged. American politics in the last thirty years has been led by social liberals of financially affluent heritage. The cynic might suggest that some of these men have tried to purge a guilty conscience, but the rest of us can rejoice that social vision has been evident in men with prestige, stability, and savoir faire. It is not easy to dismiss as reckless someone born of high stock and endowed with great wealth when he seeks social reforms of far-reaching consequence, though it is still possible to hurl against such persons invective of venomous characteristics. The bitterness of the venom may compensate for the lack of cogency in the argument.

The Biblical prophet is an earnest member of the same community of faith that he criticizes. He speaks from within a loyalty to the same covenant shared by the group brought under his judgment. The prophets are frequently admonished to peddle their complaints against the non-covenantal nations—against the "pagans" who obviously need it. They reject such advice on the grounds that reform begins within the chosen and obligated nation. The foreign powers may act unwittingly as the rod of the Lord's anger, but the prophets bring divine judgment to the household of faith. This peculiar stance of the prophet makes his role difficult since he preaches to a group that feels exempt from his criticisms or at least less properly a target than other groups. Jesus observed that a prophet is not without honor except in his own household.

The motives of men in defending existing orders or in seeking their transformation and even overturn are seldom pure. The opposing group can bolster its own case by showing that its challengers are men of bad faith or poor reputation. Demagogic smears and hysterical outcries abound in social struggle. Any cause can be attacked in this manner, for around any cause, be it a good cause or a bad one, there are bound to rally men of questionable intent and less than honorable motives. To require of any movement for historical change that it be conducted by the angels is to demand the impossible. To cultivate among people the feeling that a cause supported by men of questionable intentions and compromised virtue must be shunned is to utilize one of the most effective techniques yet devised for the thwarting of social change.

Not only do the defenders of the *status quo* find it advantageous to shift their battle line from the substantive issues at stake in a social change to the motives of its advocates—but they portray their own motives in idealistic terms. Any attempt to establish a code to eliminate discrimination in housing on the basis of race, religion, or national origin is likely to be attacked on idealistic rather than cynical grounds. It will be opposed as an unjustified attack upon the privacy of individual ownership. Seldom will people bluntly admit their prejudice and blatantly state their determination to keep housing segregated. Instead, they argue for "freedom"—meaning freedom from the extension of legal sanction to this area of community concern. Sometimes they will attack the advocates of such a petition as professional do-gooders, but more often they will pose themselves as the defenders of constitutional rights.

The self that rationalizes its own position by cloaking it in a pose of virtue when in reality it is a means of preserving power or privilege is flirting with hypocrisy and sham. There is a refreshing integrity in cynicism. Acknowledged self-interest may be more honest than appeal to abstract ideals. The overt motives here do not count: the hypocrisy need not be felt to be real. It is possible to delude the self into believing that its motives are pure. Few men advance arguments they do not really believe, but many men use arguments they have made themselves believe because they are advantageous to their own self-interest. The warnings against riches we find sprinkled throughout the New Testament are warnings against the subtle erosions of moral sensitivity that occur when the "heart" is placed in bondage to influences that delude it and dilute its capacity for self-critical appraisal.

But challengers of the existing order are no less prone to excess, pretension, and sham than its defenders. The social revolutionary may feel that his thrust for rights and status stems from devotion to a noble cause, but his motives in struggle may be compounded of many other drives. They may be selfish—driven by the craving to get something that benefits his own group or class; they may be neurotic —seeking a thrilling cause in which to bury personal frustration and through which to obtain escape for the self that is unable to adjust to normal responsibility; they may be vengeful—seeking to get even with those who have subjugated him in the past.

Our world is full of revolutionary movements driven by the pent-up hatreds of long years of subjugation. Many of these movements arise in underdeveloped countries long exploited by Western imperialism; others exist among colored nations long the brunt of white arrogance. These movements will not be daunted in their thrust for status even though in many instances they have not yet achieved the structural capacity to create their own orders of stability. They are not responsive to a meliorism that begs for the chance to set things right through deliberate planning, nor do they hesitate to substitute one system of oppression for another. Other groups stand in dread of their portent, unappreciative of the motives that lie behind the revolutionary thrust, and dedicated to forceful resistance of all their aims.

A small yet alarming movement of Black Nationalism has arisen in the United States that illustrates the extremity of a previously exploited group. The patience of the majority Negro community with our long-delayed achievement of equal opportunity is one of the marvels of contemporary history, but the Black Muslims would turn the tables instead of righting the scales. Here is an exerpt from a sermon preached in Harlem's Temple of Islam No. 7 and reported by the pastor of a Christian church in Harlem.

You are a lost race! [In Africa] . . . you were there in the seeds of your forebears—proud, hard-working, happy! Handsome black men! Beautiful black women! White John Hawkins came among you, posing as a friend. For over forty years, he lived in your trust, spinning you tales of milk and honey in North America! You still trusted when he sailed a cargo of you to Jamestown on his ship. *Jesus* was the name of that ship! Proud, strong, beautiful black people! Sons and daughters of Ham! A people whose rich heritage down through time has known kings, heroes, nobility! White man's histories don't tell you what! White John Hawkins! His good ship *Jesus!* Beginning a white devil industry! Tearing noble human beings from their rich, black Africa to be North America's slaves! (Callender, Eugene S., "Black Nationalism," *Union Seminary Quarterly Review,* March, 1962, p. 208. Used by permission.)

Frightening as this may sound, is it any more frightening than statements of a similar tone that come from the defenders of segregation and white supremacy? There is thunder on both the left and right. Here, for example, is a paragraph from a pamphlet describing the White Citizens' Council:

The fate of our great nation may well rest in the hands of the Southern white people today. If we submit to this unconstitutional, judge-made integration law, the malignant power of atheism, communism, and mongrelization will surely follow, not only in our Southland but throughout our nation. To falter would be tragic; to fail would be fatal. The white people of the South will again stand fast and preserve an unsullied race as our forefathers did eighty years ago. We will not be integrated, either suddenly or gradually. (From pamphlet published by the Association of White Citizens' Councils of Mississippi, p. 3.)

The irresistible force and the immovable object are fictions of the imagination, but the Black Muslims and the White Citizens would play the roles if they could. If such attitudes remain minority movements within a cushion of softer attitudes, we can hope for healthy and eventual social change, but if one or both become the dominant mood in either the defense or challenge of the *status quo,* only violence and agony can result. Gunpowder is most explosive when it is tightly packed.

Unfortunately, loyalty to cause is greater among extremists than among the rank and file of sensible citizens. Such movements create centers of unreserved loyalty that further develop their own intransigence. When this happens the nature of partisanship is transformed into idolatry, and struggle over moral issues becomes a devotion to value-absolutes.

VI

IDOLATRY AND PARTISANSHIP: THE ENIGMA OF MORALE

MEN struggle because they believe in a cause, and they struggle most ardently when such a belief is at a fever pitch. A set of sustaining convictions is necessary for morale. Without the engendering enthusiasm of a cause, men can quickly drift toward defeat. The intensity of men's loyalty for a cause may even be more crucial in determining their zeal than the inherent value of the end they seek. Fanatics are born more readily from total devotions to petty causes than from half-hearted allegiance to great objectives.

Every participant in struggle naturally tends to look upon his cause as worthy of the effort needed to sustain it. No man wants to struggle for that which seems trivial or to expend his life for that which he deems fruitless. Only when a person is convinced that momentous issues are at stake—which includes those instances in which small issues are considered momentous—do his passions rise and his enthusiasms grow to the point where he can successfully conduct a battle against an adversary or endure the rigors related to the conquest of the elements. The man who would struggle to win must convince himself and his associates that his cause is crucial and victory necessary. Barring such a conviction, there may be little zeal to win.

In his study of mass movements—movements responsible for rapid and significant social change—Eric Hoffer suggests that "some kind of widespread enthusiasm or excitement is apparently needed for the realization of vast and rapid change, and it does not seem to matter whether the exhilaration is derived from an expectation of untold riches or is generated by an active mass movement" (*The True Believer,* p. 3). Hoffer calls the individual who is fired with passion for a cause a "true believer" and describes his fanatical faith and readiness to die for what he considers a holy cause. If this diagnosis holds, the convictional intensity of a participant in struggle is a larger factor in the determination of his zeal than the nobility of the cause for which he desires success.

Intense commitment to a cause usually depends upon a conviction that the cause is just and good. Other elements enter, to be sure, for morale is also dependent upon a sight of victory and a sense of strategic hopefulness. The degree of devotion—its quantitative intensity—to a cause evidenced in a struggling group seems the major source of its drive and the largest sustainer of its efforts. This devotion cannot be had without an inner conviction on the part of the group that its cause is right and its efforts worthy. The group may not be correct in its assessment of the issues but it must think that it is. Perverse loyalties are tragically common even though sham enthusiasm is difficult to sustain. Men may be impelled to sacrifice an effort based upon ardent belief in wrong things but they are not likely to sustain at length sacrifices that inwardly they consider uncalled for.

The moral base that groups attribute to the causes for which they struggle gathers around it more moral pretension than is justified. What often starts as a minor effort to achieve a legitimate but truly proximate objective turns into a venture of ultimate significance. When the United States entered the First World War, partly at least in anger over the sinking of a ship, it ballooned its purposes into "making the world safe for democracy." The slogan sustained morale, but hardly embraced the realities of the situation—as subsequent experience has sadly demonstrated. The Second World War was begun in anger over the bombing of a naval base but was finally sustained by the cry for "unconditional surrender." Convinced that the total annihilation of the offending nations would somehow remove political evil from history, the nation fought less to avenge Pearl Harbor than to eradicate treachery from international affairs.

Unqualified loyalty to cause is found on all levels of conflict. Robert Jungk reports a visit to a modern chemical research laboratory conducting experiments for products to be marketed twenty years in the future. His guide, a chemist enmeshed in the activities, conducted him with the one-sided exuberance that marks an outfit with high morale. The wonder products under development were looked at one by one: nonfreezing oil, cool synthetics for hot climates and warm synthetics for cold ones, and an artificial light-emitting building material. Remarking about the chemist's obvious enthusiasm, Jungk makes the following report:

He said all this without for a moment seeming a visionary or a braggart. He was as sure of the future as the self-righteous are of the Kingdom of Heaven. Although he was employed by a firm which had begun with the production of gunpowder, expanded during the First World War by the manufacture of high explosives, had built the Plutonium Works at Hanford in the Second World War, and was now, on commission from the Government, equipping the first hydrogen bomb factory on the Savannah River, the Du Pont researcher apparently did not include the possibility of a catastrophic war in his calculations. He was on terms of intimate familiarity with tomorrow and the day after. If that which was to come held terrors for him, he gave no sign of it. (*Tomorrow Is Already Here*, p. 222.)

Not to display high enthusiasm for all types and forms of scientific investigation is a kind of nonconformity that may even be considered by some as a kind of heresy. One of America's large manufacturers conducts a television program that uses as its motto: "Progress Is Our Most Important Product." What might happen if one of the guests were to argue that the slogan should become "Wisdom Is Our Most Important Attainment"? Think of the shudder that would be created in the audience if the announcer misread his script and observed that "Redemption Is Man's Most Crucial Need"! Even to qualify the value of scientific endeavor by noting its ambiguous nature, its unleashing of fears as well as its bestowal of blessings, its costs as well as its benefits, seems to many people the most blatant kind of disloyalty to the most creative enterprise in our time.

Or consider the conflict over desegregation. The sit-in demonstrators speak of their unwillingness "to co-operate with evil," or of "the struggle between justice and injustice." They see the "forces of light arrayed against the forces of darkness" or suggest that "the isness of segregation has not the oughtness of moral law." Because these phrases cast the issues into antinomies and seem to justify any acts done to achieve desegregation, Paul Ramsey calls them to task. Such phrases, according to Ramsey, "should not be allowed to obscure Christian responsibility for the purely impersonal context of a legal system which alone makes possible any life of sinful man with sinful man." (*Christian Ethics and the Sit-in,* pp. 77 f.)

On the other side we see the defenders of segregation producing their own one-sided forms of zeal. In a pamphlet about White Citizens' Councils already cited we read:

People with racial pride are attacked by the NAACP and its affiliates as being bigoted, prejudiced, biased, immoral, un-American, etc. These hysterical smear words are used in lieu of any logical reason why a person can no longer be loyal to his white blood, his church, his state, and his nation above all else.

In other words, the right to *esprit de corps,* which has won every war we have fought, is no longer in style. The idea now is seemingly to pride ourselves in the fact that everybody in the world should be made equal by law regardless of aptitude or heritage. The "have nots" must share equally with the "have gots" in the new world order. (*The Citizens' Council,* p. 2.)

General Leslie Groves once remarked that "a properly trained soldier does not have to be convinced of the righteousness of his cause" (*The New York Times,* May 27, 1961, p. 10). According to Groves a soldier can fight without knowing why. He does so if he has learned to trust his superiors and obey their orders. A soldier's effectiveness is undercut if he concerns himself too much with philosophical analysis of his purposes. To "think of both sides of a question" only destroys clarity of purpose. To ask why one is fighting is to divert attention from how one expects to win. Groves did not refute the thesis of this chapter by arguing against the need for causes—but proposed a cause that could demand unconditional response on an immediate level—implicit trust in the leadership of the Armed Forces. Morale is dependent upon *esprit de corps,* which in turn is based upon obedience to the outfit, upon unquestioning and unreflective participation in the military venture itself. Groves simply described a common way of maintaining morale by keeping partisanship simplified: men transfer their dedication from noble moral objectives to the group that professes to support them. Not theirs to reason why—especially if such reasoning turns up a sense of ambiguity in the moral status of the enterprise. It is easiest to do and die if nobody asks many questions.

Caught in the enthusiastic response of vivacious commitment, the soldier is prepared for rigor and sacrifice and may display extraordinary measures of courage. Military life frequently elicits the highest kind of loyalty from men. It even surrounds itself with genuine dimensions of moral grandeur, bringing forth not only heroism and sacrifice but willingness on the part of men to work as a team. In calling for a moral equivalent of war William James seized upon the significance of such moral attainments in the hope that they could be sublimated for constructive use.

Service in the military may become an object of devotion to which many people give an unexamined priority. Consider, for example, how many individuals honor the enlistee or draftee but suspect the Peace Corps worker. How many Congressmen have adamantly insisted that service in the latter must not become an alternative for the former? Presupposing that work in the Peace Corps is fully as demanding and unpleasant as service in the Armed Forces—and probably as hazardous—what is the significance of this attitude? Must all men serve in the same way unless that way has gathered around it a claim and significance denied to other means of meeting the world situation? By what configuration of loyalties, other than a process in which the military venture has become an end in itself, do we ignore a variety of services in response to the crises of our day?

A sense of loyalty to a group or utter abandon to a cause seems intimately related to the achievement of high morale. In a paper distributed by Dr. J. H. Irvine, President of the Riverdale Mental Health Association, Dr. William C. Menninger, of Topeka, Kansas, has written:

> It seems to me so important in terms of the effectiveness of the folks associated with us . . . [that we develop] our own thoughtful consideration of how to motivate people—the essentiality of seeing to it that we have a group that in the final analysis thinks that it is "the best damn outfit in the Army." Not the attitude that, "I only work here." In the Army, where through motivation that kind of morale was created, we never had to worry about psychiatric casualties and, what's more,

we knew that the outfit was doing a good job. Invariably that was the case. In contrast, there were many, many times when, because of poor leadership plus sometimes many other factors that made for extreme difficulty, we found the fellows, in the vernacular of the Army that you well recall, were "browned off." There we always had lots of psychiatric casualties.

Any detached and disinterested observer knows quite clearly that the average soldier does not, and cannot, belong to the "best damn outfit in the Army." There is only one outfit that could possibly be "best," and its weaknesses in some areas might offset its strengths in others. The substantive truth of the situation is not crucial; a soldier needs only to believe that his outfit is the best in order to bolster his morale. He needs only believe he is doing a good job in order to increase his enthusiasm for it.

There is a negative counterpart to these observations. Not only must the positive results of one's own actions be painted in the most glowing terms, but the enemy must be painted in the blackest. Not only do men delude themselves concerning the virtue and necessity of their cause in order to pursue it with zeal but they also make anathema the position of their enemies. How else are we to understand the governor of a Southern state when he remarks: "All Georgians know that the Federal Courts are moving swiftly against Southern thought and culture and that they are doing so with a viciousness peculiar only to tyranny and dictatorship"? (*The New York Times*, January 10, 1961, p. 22.)

The questions raised by these observations can be sharply put: Must men be deluded in order to win? Does success in struggle depend upon the idolatry that turns a proximate value into an object of total devotion? Must men's expectations from victory be inflated beyond all possible accomplishment in order for them to deem the victory worth pursuing? Must their allegiance to their outfit—platoon, division, club, or party—ignore its weaknesses and swell their pride before they are willing to dig in and do a decent job? Must men become idolaters in order to be effective partisans?

It may be a tribute to the influence of the Hebrew-Christian tradition in our culture that we behave as partisans of absolutes, for in the religious heritage of our culture exclusive and unfettered loyalty to God is demanded of the believer. Dilution and qualification are anathema. Our modern culture has learned the lesson about the nature of such loyalty better than it has learned that God alone is a proper object for it. When the singleness of devotion that is required for worship of the true God is transferred to a lesser object of devotion the most subtle and most acute forms of idolatry arise. To be unreservedly loyal to the wrong object of confidence is a more dangerous condition than to be incapable of unreserved loyalty, since it paves the way for turning cultural relativities into functional substitutes for obedience to the one true Absolute.

It is for this reason that the prophets were suspicious of religious faith for its own sake. If idolatry is most possible when struggle is taken most seriously and reaches an apex when moral dimensions are taken most absolutely, must we not be suspicious of religious faith intertwined with worldly struggles? Religion may increase the vigor of idolatry. Culture-faiths of fighting groups usually cloak the most blatant forms of false allegiance. Hence, a prophet may even call for the abolition of "religious" institutions in order that a nation might be brought back to a dependent relationship with its covenantal God.

Consider the possibility that we might need to reformulate our typical attitude toward participation in struggle. We tend to regard the cynical politician who manufactures statements of moral ideals for purely propaganda purposes as a contemptible example of bad faith. His tongue-in-check attitude makes him a schemer, a cynical manipulator of power and influence, an opportunist who stops at nothing to gain his way. But at least he knows what he is doing and is less a victim of delusion than his self-righteous counterpart who has come to believe his own platform and is under the illusion that he will carry it through as soon as elected. There may be a provisional virtue in the position of the cynical manipulator of power and influence, a virtue lacking in the deluded and self-righteous crusader. The mercenary may be less in danger of idolatry than the strident patriot. Both, in a negative way, avoid the absolutizing of a partial virtue. As between cynicism and self-delusion the former may actually be nearer to wisdom— though fortunately there is another possibility.

Partisanship is idolatrous in proportion to the degree that it erases doubt concerning the legitimacy of one's own cause. Every human purpose is ambiguous, a mixture of good and evil intentions and constructive and destructive consequences. To ignore the evil and to overplay the good, especially to the point where the good is made into an absolute, is not only to be guilty of moral insensitivity but of spiritual malallegiance. To postulate the triumph of virtue as equivalent with the success of one's own cause is to court the false absolutism that makes participation in conflict spiritually dangerous.

This kind of loyalty is by no means the exclusive trait of any one side in a conflict. Both sides of every issue tend to claim more righteousness for their cause than the situation warrants. This is true of all conflict, be the weapons violent and the rituals performed with flags, or the means employed nonviolent and the rituals performed with prayers. Anyone who has witnessed a wartime argument between a pacifist preacher and a nonpacifist congregation over the positioning of the national emblem in relation to the flag of the Christian church, or over the church's respective attitudes toward sons in service with the military and sons in civilian public service ought to appreciate the extent to which men's loyalties in time of conflict become the engrossing emotive drives of their lives.

Complete abandon to a cause breeds an inward resentment against those who criticize or qualify it. There are few quicker devices for incurring the wrath of men than to criticize their roles in struggle. Such criticism is especially unwelcome from within the group against which it is aimed. In our day, traitors are treated with greater disdain and malicious fortune than heretics, but both are subject to scorn for their unwillingness to go along with the loyalties of the group. Critics suffer similar disdain in milder degrees, especially in cultures so immature that they cannot understand the meaning of his majesty's loyal opposition or the contribution of the minority to healthy government.

Some men would compensate for the false absolutisms that spring from enthusiastic loyalties by ignoring the moral distinctions between the two sides in a dispute. By crying "a plague on both your houses" they achieve transcendence at the price of removal from the arena of conflict. This may even take the form of whitewashing the evils of an enemy in order to counteract self-righteousness among one's compatriots. But it is ridiculous to suppose that because there is evil in both sides of a conflict that the contest between them involves no moral consequences worth defending or seeking. True discrimination is needed —a discrimination that admits the weakness in one's own cause as well as decides which of several proximate values demands actual support. To settle for a proximate victory with gratitude for small gains and to hold one's own side under prophetic scrutiny and vigilance demand a kind of maturity and perspective all too scarce in a day of total war and political self-righteousness.

It is easy for Americans to criticize the complete devotion of the communist to the movement of which he is a part. His willingness to take his thinking from the party, to determine both his behavior and his means of justifying it from the official line, is an example of unreserved commitment to a limited, and from our perspective, a perverse commitment. The party plays the functional role of "god" and the ideology of the group furnishes the creedal system by which the loyalty is justified. But the behavior of the communist at this point has many precedents and significant parallels in the behavior of men in the noncommunist portions of the world. Even those who break with communism may espouse their anticommunism with the same fanatical devotion they once gave to the Marxist cause. "The messianic intellectual," writes Everett Knight, "like the believer, needs a world in which Right and Wrong are clean-contoured and clearly labelled." (*The Objective Society,* p. 11. Routledge & Kegan Paul, Ltd., London, 1959.)

It should not have taken the rise of communism to teach us that fanatical devotion to specific causes is not a trait appearing only in the avowedly religious. We are describing a general kind of human behavior, not merely one induced by a fanaticism created by theistic faith. Indeed, it is fair to ask whether any major enthusiasm of widespread influence has appeared in a purely religious form in Western culture in recent decades. The messianisms and fanaticisms of our century have been political rather than religious in nature, though religion is involved with many as a useful tool of the more dynamic forces of mass movements.

In September of 1959 the Moral Re-Armament movement distributed millions of copies of a pamphlet entitled *Ideology and Co-existence.* The pamphlet is dedicated to the creation of ideological enthusiasm against the spread of communism, and suggests that only with strong devotion—unqualified commitment—to the cause of the free world is there a chance for victory in the struggle of the cold war. It quotes with implied approval a speech made at its headquarters by a former official in the Communist Party of Canada. In the speech we find both the call for complete devotion and the warning against compromise that is characteristic of ardent crusaders:

> It burns me up to see our business leaders trotting off to Moscow for brainwashing and then coming back to try to brainwash the rest of us without even realizing what they are doing.
>
> If the leadership of the free world is sincerely interested in saving civilization, they will come to Mackinac, which is the only place in the free world where anybody can be equipped with a moral ideology. The choice is Moscow or Mackinac. (P. 15.)

In the same work earlier quoted, Everett Knight suggests that "the fanaticism of the illiterate is but the other face of the intellectual's need for the spiritual comfort of final answers" (p. 10). In the pamphlet of the Moral Re-Armament movement, Eudocio Ravines, a former Communist, has this to say: "There is need for an ideology—a superior thinking that will satisfy the hunger for the absolute which burns in the heart of the illiterate and the educated alike." (P. 27.) Ravines seems to be calling for more of the very spiritual attitude Knight is decrying. This debate between the printed pages of unrelated books sharpens the questions before us. Is dilution of commitment the beginning of humble wisdom or an invitation to defeat? Can men successfully struggle against social evil without creating a new form of evil, a form of evil bred of men's fanatical allegiance to goodness rather than of their demonstration of perversity?

If any good cause can be successfully supported by the mere creation of enthusiasm for it and if fanatical devotion brings valid victories, then it may be argued that all necessary means to create dynamic mass movements dedicated to the right purposes are justified. But if the fanatical level of devotion oversteps its task and spoils by excess the purposes it hopes to serve, then we should seek for more than reckless abandon cultivated by unreflective and unqualified commitment to a cause. There must be more to victory in struggle than successful destruction of an opponent; there must be the creation of a climate in which the intentions and values of the victor are worthy of continued expression, and the values of the vanquished are allowed to reappear.

When winning becomes an end in itself struggle is corrupted. Lewis Mumford has noted what happens to sport when it is part of a prestige scramble.

Sport, then, in this mechanized society, is no longer a mere game empty of any reward other than the playing: it is a profitable business: millions are invested in arenas, equipment, and players, and the maintenance of sport becomes as important as the maintenance of any other form of profit-making mechanism. And the technique of mass-sport infects other activities: scientific expeditions and geographical explorations are conducted in the manner of a speed stunt or a prizefight—*and for the same reason*. (*Technics and Civilization*, p. 307. Harcourt, Brace and World, 1934. Used by permission.)

When alumni will not cheer unless the team is winning or contribute unless it succeeds in getting a bid to some famous bowl, the sense of victory has destroyed the sense of sport.

Speaking of another form of struggle, George F. Kennan has remarked:

It is a curious thing, but it is true, that the legalistic approach to world affairs, rooted as it unquestionably is in a desire to do away with war and violence, makes violence more enduring, more terrible, and more destructive to political stability than did the older motives of national interest. A war fought in the name of high moral principle finds no early end short of some form of total domination. . . .

There is no more dangerous delusion, none that has done us a greater disservice in the past or threatens to do us a greater disservice in the future, than the concept of total victory. (*American Diplomacy: 1900–1950*, pp. 101 f. The University of Chicago Press. Copyright 1951 by The University of Chicago.)

Kennan presupposes that the thrust for total victory, a thrust expressed by slogans such as "unconditional surrender" and "making the world safe for democracy" is born from an attempt to eradicate evil from history. Perhaps these slogans are born from another, somewhat less obvious, motive—to provide men with a cause so great they will have no hesitation to fight for it. One of the lessons of the Korean War was a realization that men lack a sense of satisfaction fighting a limited war for limited objectives under self-imposed restraints.

The very kind of self-transcending doubt that is needed to preserve men from moral pretension and spiritual idolatry of their own cause would seem to undercut their zeal to win. When General Groves observes that a soldier who is worried about two sides of a question may not fight well, he poses a genuine problem. Higher zeals are most quickly sustained among those who regard their cause as totally just and unambiguous. If morale is dependent upon unqualified allegiance to the cause for which a person fights, idolatry may be the price of success. If a war effort must be immune from criticism, if political activity must be intensely partisan, if the game must be played as a business —is there any possible chance of maintaining just proportions in the fray?

Ethical relativism, cynical disillusionment, and indifference to the outcomes of historical encounter certainly avoid the false inflation of a partial value. But they purchase freedom from a false commitment by ruling out the possibility of true commitment. As between utter surrender to a cause and cynical indifference posing as a false sophistication; as between an ethical absolutism that over-simplifies issues in order to dramatize virtues and an ethical indifference to the issues at stake in struggle; as between an ideological enthusiasm that grows stronger than some forms of religious devotion itself and a complacent tolera-tion of conflicting schemes of value—we cannot expect that good will come by choosing one or the other side. If we embrace idolatry to avoid apostasy, we stay as far from living encounter with God as if we embrace indifference to avoid fanaticism.

This chapter ends with diagnosis, since other chapters follow to explore the possibility that prophetic religious faith can extricate us from the horns of the dilemma. We have already said that many destructive postures in human struggle are intensified by religious zeal, for what passes for religion is frequently nothing but the projection to higher levels of commitment of all the divisive realities of men's partisan strivings. By cloaking the unpleasantries of struggle with pious sanctities religion has frequently blasphemed its calling; by making the pursuit of partial virtue into unconditional crusades religion has frequently placed churchly sanction upon that deserving of divine judgment; by confusing loyalty to God with allegiance to a limited cause religion has compounded the idolatry of partisanship beyond normal human arrogance. The mere embrace of religion can actually be an obstacle rather than an aid in transforming struggle from a destructive to a more creative aspect of human life.

But to regard all religion as similar in nature or iden-tical in consequence is grossly to oversimplify the analysis. Religions differ in both the content and the consequences of their loyalties. Priestly religion has sometimes en-trenched the *status quo* and earned the just ire of the forward-looking observer, yet prophetic religion has upset established orders at the point of their corruption and

earned the unjust enmity of those in power. Legalistic religion has sometimes made the self-styled righteous more
self-righteous than they might have been without holy
zeal, but religions of judgment, forgiveness, and grace have
also humbled men and put down the proud from their
perches. Not to distinguish between the differing forms of
religious understanding is inexcusable sloth, or a form of
pseudointellectual scapegoating that seeks to ignore com-
plexities by finding simple alibis to explain them away.

It is therefore unfair to suggest that religion creates
more problems than it solves in the working of the social
order. It is no more legitimate to reject the contribution
of religion prior to scrutiny than it is to affirm its contribution immune from examination. Hostile rejection is
less guilty of premature conclusions than uncritical defense. Certain types of religious belief and practice may
contribute sorrowfully to the intensification of the problems related to struggle, but other forms may contribute
promisingly to its transformation. It is the theme of the
argument that follows that the creative function of religion is best expressed in a prophetically self-critical variety
of faith that uses yet transforms the vitalities within which
it works—and does this because its loyalty to God is set in
judgment over human loyalties which threaten to become
absolute.

VII

THE JUSTIFICATION OF THE SELF
AND THE EMBRACE OF THE OTHER:
THE AMELIORATION OF STRUGGLE

THE suggestions that follow
presume a particular religious outlook. Its label is not
important though the content is. What has been said in
diagnosis of struggle cannot be divorced from what is
about to be said concerning its amelioration. The analysis
of struggle made in the preceding material is fully infused
with the perspective of faith itself. Since faith is the perspective from which all of life is viewed and not merely a
device employed to pull men from a mire, the form of
analysis is fully as much a work of faith as the proposal of
a cure. Faith must insist that the questions are framed in
proper form, the problems understood in proper perspective, the difficulties perceived in a fruitful fashion. To
leave the formulation of the issues to independent human
reason, then to expect that the answers formulated from
the perspective of faith will fit, is utter foolishness. Therefore, in moving from analysis to prescription we move
from one function of faith to another and not from modes
of thinking in which faith plays no role to modes of thinking in which it alone is functional.

We have argued that struggle tempts the self to seek its
security by the intended destruction of the other. We have
gone on to suggest that struggle intensifies the insecurity of

108

the self even while seeking to establish its security. Prophetic religious faith asserts that the only ultimate security available to the self is the security that comes from acceptance by a loving God. This security is a gift rather than an attainment; it is accepted rather than achieved. It is a gift because it comes from God and cannot be created or sustained by men.

This gift is not a banal substitute for tensions, nor does it come for glib asking. It is costly because the conditions of acceptance involve the surrender of a self that otherwise thrusts toward the procurement of its own security. Acceptance of this gift is difficult because the self must acknowledge its need and a successful self is apt to find the necessity of acknowledgment even more difficult than does the failing self. Acts of repentance and surrender appropriate to the acceptance of forgiving love run counter to those acts of self-assertiveness frequently associated with the struggle for status and security. The self accustomed to maintain a front is hard pressed when forced to acknowledge its need of help. For this reason properly to accept an unmerited gift is an even greater art than proudly to attain a virtue—and just as costly.

Whereas in struggle the self lunges for a security procured by strength and therefore tries to hide its weakness, in surrender to God the self is given security at the point where it acknowledges its need most honestly. When the self is striving to prove its strength it is difficult for it to accept a gift that is acquired by acknowledging weakness. The individual whose relationships to nature, to peers, and to strangers require him to prove his superiority to others finds that about-face required in his relationship to God almost impossible to execute. The inability to trust the self to God is normal and natural in a world of struggle, but it blocks the only ultimate channel for the transformation of struggle into a tolerable aspect of human experience.

It is not surprising that many forms of religious belief merely provide a new channel for the self to prove its strength and display its virtue. They look upon the religious life as men look upon the life of struggle—as challenge and demand. They involve the self in new forms of struggle by demanding moral rectitude and spiritual concentration. In addition to the struggles with nature and neighbor such religion sets up a new struggle between the self and God. Man is placed under yet another tension rather than relieved of his existing ones. The religious ingredient merely projects to new heights the problems of the old depths.

In personal terms the heightened tension appears as the effort to do enough to please God; in social terms it appears as the effort to make others over into our own image. When, misguided by zeal, men take upon themselves to oversee the morals of their fellowmen, they create new tensions and bitter divisions among their neighbors. The attempts to goad others to goodness run the gamut from the sorry efforts of old-maidish prigs to the self-righteous machinations of Grand Inquisitors. Not content to strive merely for the attainment of their own virtue those impelled by the struggle to be righteous attempt to police the morals of the world. In moderate instances this process only proves annoying, but in the extreme case it crucifies the man of higher goodness and profounder virtue than is understood by the moral policeman. Such a perversion always springs from a religious outlook that makes spiritual struggle for the attainment of goodness the final preoccupation of the faithful man, not only in regard to personal behavior but in his relationship to the life of his social groupings.

Men of such temperament may lead great crusades by bullying the submissive allegiance of other men but they cannot create the healing patterns of genuine community.

In the world's eyes they may succeed but inwardly they may be ill at ease and yearning for the chance to do something that makes them feel secure in their attainment. They relate themselves to others by destroying the initiative and independence of their companions, by rewarding conformity and surrender rather than individuality and growth. Their relationship to others seems secure only when they feel superior enough to others to sense no threat, but since their overbearing is resented, it only magnifies the insecurity.

When the self is obsessed with the effort to attain renown there is no level of attainment that can satisfy its cravings because there is always a higher possible level of success to which the anxious self can aspire. But when life is understood as a meaningful service to God, all levels of attainment have significance because they are meaningful as part of that service. Those who know that they are loved by God will find every level of accomplishment—high success or lowly dedication—an occasion of meaning and even a source of joy.

Jesus Christ was able to transform the relationship of the virtuous Jew to sinful outcasts because he was himself secure in relationship to God. Whereas the Pharisees shunned tax collectors and sinners in order to preserve their own purity, Jesus welcomed their company in order to preach them his message. Jesus was able to accept even the woman taken in adultery, since he had no need to prove his virtue by stoning her for her actions. Even when he became the object of persecution and was hailed before the tribunal, he was, in Harry Emerson Fosdick's description, "the one calm man in Pilate's court."

Likewise, the apostle Paul, in dealing with the thorny problem as to whether Christians should eat meat that came from the idol worship of pagan temples insisted that the decision be made on the grounds of helpfulness for the brethren and not on the grounds of what is necessary for the self to show its virtue. Secure enough to eat or not eat, Paul made up his mind on the basis of his brothers' need rather than in an effort to police the behavior of everyone else.

Luther, standing before his accusers at Worms, replied to them with neither rancor nor compromise. Roland Bainton translates his final reply in this way:

Since then Your Majesty and your lordships desire a simple reply, I will answer without horns and without teeth. Unless I am convinced by Scripture and plain reason—I do not accept the authority of popes and councils, for they have contradicted each other—my conscience is captive to the Word of God. I cannot and will not recant anything, for to go against conscience is neither right nor safe. God help me. Amen. (*Here I Stand*, p. 185. Abingdon Press, 1950. Used by permission.)

Many of us could wish that Luther's secure poise before the officials in this debate had remained characteristic in all his subsequent life. When Luther ceased to be persecuted and achieved some status he opposed the peasants in their revolt with the kind of bitterness he himself had experienced. It is a temptation to abandon Luther as an illustration of concern for neighbor, but he represents yet another and crucial truth. Men who act greatly in one situation may betray themselves in another. The greatness is not thereby canceled because the individual has not been able to achieve it in all situations. The human response to the creative love of God is not worthless because its receipt is subject to perversion, nor does the case for religious maturity depend upon its total attainment by all men who profess to seek it. Luther could write movingly of the grace to neighbor that flows from the experienced grace of God. His words express that which all Christians, including Luther himself, seek in hope.

From faith flows love and joy in the Lord, and from love a joyful, willing and free mind that serves one's neighbor willingly and takes no account of gratitude or ingratitude, of praise or blame, of gain or loss. For a man does not serve that he may put men under obligations, he does not distinguish between friends and enemies, nor does he anticipate their thankfulness or unthankfulness, but most freely and willingly he spends himself and all that he has, whether he wastes all on the thankless or whether he gains a reward. . . . As our heavenly father has in Christ freely come to our help, we also ought freely to help our neighbor through our body and its works, and each should become as it were a Christ to the other, that we may be Christs to one another and Christ may be the same in all. (*A Treatise on Christian Liberty*, Holman edition, Vol. II, p. 338.)

Many of the problems we have attributed to the presence of struggle in human life can be mitigated only by the kind of reoriented selfhood created by the religious experience of justification. The only ultimate security available to the self is the acceptance by a loving God known through faith, though the self can make lesser securities functionally ultimate for limited purposes and limited periods of time. Whereas struggle seeks to enhance the security of the self by destroying the competitor, religious faith by obtaining security for the self from dependence upon a God who cares and concerns himself with men enables men to embrace others in the security of God's embrace of them. "We love, because he first loved us." (I John 4:19.)

This is the point at which individual wholeness and social responsibility become interrelated. The relationship of the self to God is more profound when it includes the social dimension and ingredients of transformed struggle than when it approaches salvation as the attainment of a highly individualistic and essentially quietistic Nirvana. The same self is ready to be poured out toward its neighbor in compassion and healing, since it can avoid those spiritual imperialisms that sow dissension between men. Any dichotomy between individual redemption and social salvation is as false in theory as it is perverse when found in practice.

The healing work of religious faith has different overtones in each of the three forms of struggle, but there is a basic note that relates each to the other. The self that seeks security through striving finds justification from God and in turn embraces rather than seeks to destroy the other. This occurs, not as something added to the experiences of struggle or as an escape from it, but as a way of understanding and relating the self to the realities in which it is embroiled. Religious salvation is not an alternative to life itself but a different way of embracing it.

Competition destroys community when the individual self becomes ultimately concerned about its own success and status. Concern about salary and money may be one measure of enslavement, but more frequently concern about salary and money is sublimated by the claims of the family that is supported by them. Concern about status and prestige is a more sinister measure of enslavement to the competitive life, since prestige is of benefit to almost no one other than the self. When the security of the self is sought by means of money or prestige every setback corrodes the spirit and every failure to climb the ladder of success becomes a bitter disenchantment.

Suppose that the tense inhabitant of the split-level suburban home discovers through prayerful experience that the meaning of his life can be viewed in terms of a relational surrender to God rather than in terms of his attainments in the hierarchy of his business life. He may even get such an insight from a grossly oversimplified "peace of mind" sermon at his local church—though the chances are that such a sermon will relax the tensions rather than shift the object of ultimate concern. He may be tempted to turn his back upon the way of life represented by the office rat race—to make a heroic demonstration of surrender to God involving, for example, the taking of a mission post in some distant land. He may be tempted to use a supposed trust in God to support and sustain his enthusiasm for life so as to guarantee success in the scramble of which he is a part. But hopefully, he may find a new perspective on the present enterprise, re-embrace it with candor and tentativeness rather than rancor and bitter seriousness, riding the momentary turns of fortune with confidence that his selfhood has a rootage that transcends the achievements or failures of the moment. In this case his religious faith will enable him to transform struggle without running from it, and to master his uncertainties through faith without making religion into a servant of his own intent for victory.

This transcendence may take no more startling a form than frank admission about his predicament. The person who can admit his plight and laugh at himself within it is on the road to health. Indeed, the nonreligious person who learns to do this may be wiser and happier than the religious person who doesn't, and while his transcendence may be short-scoped, it can be healing. Indeed, such persons may find others who have learned to laugh as well as struggle, and can "let off steam" in the company of those who rise above their situation by refusing to let it conquer them.

That such attitudes can be found among the "nonreligious" as well as the consciously religious members of the population in no sense invalidates the contention that it can be engendered on Christian grounds and embraced in the full richness of response to God's love. It is clearly possible for men to experience a sense of acceptance on human terms that will give them the ability to laugh at themselves and embrace their neighbors without canceling the fact that the same experience can be known profoundly in terms of surrendered trust to God. Moreover, it is by no means clear that the religious individual may achieve this position more fully or more readily than others, since not all religious people appropriate the full dimensions of grace. Religious spokesmen can do great harm by portraying God's love too blandly, by claiming too easy cures for human insecurity from the divine work of justification, or by seeking to deny the dimensions of validity in human analogies to the healing work of grace.

What is true of competitive struggle is also true of conquest. The scientist who seeks to learn the secrets of nature and the explorer who travels to parts unknown in order to extend knowledge of the world (and in our day, knowledge of the space around the world) can undertake such exploration with different motives. He may become totally engrossed with the enterprise itself, carried completely away by his involvement in it, and thus lose any sense of meaning in the struggle other than the meaning implicit in his own success. Or he may embrace his task in a mood of humility—a humility that enlarges with each new discovery and enriches with every new appreciation of the vastness of the cosmos within which man lives his days and achieves his successes. The first mood breeds exploitation; the second, stewardship. The first mood seeks the "thrust to omnipotence" which makes for the secularization of struggle and a climate that eclipses God from its conscious trust; the second rejoices in the creativity that is bequeathed to man by his Creator.

It may not be possible for the lonesome believer to reverse the pattern or change the assumptions of the culture in which he works. His transcendence may be the transcendence of perception rather than of transformation—but this alone is significant for the life of faith. In a remarkably perceptive and equally candid commentary upon the scientific enterprise in our day, William G. Pollard has confessed:

For nearly a century now the whole of our Western civilization, and especially that segment of it planted in our own land, has been living under a terrible illusion through which it has been led, for the most part unsuspectingly and unknowingly, into the awful sin of total rebellion against Almighty God in a revolution that will be satisfied with nothing short of seizing all of his creation from him and making it over entirely to suit our needs and purposes rather than his. This rebellion has acquired such universal proportions and has so intimately involved every phase and component of our economic and social structure that the sheer momentum of history will sweep every one of us along with it. I myself am inextricably trapped in this movement in an especially vulnerable way. I am a physicist by training and profession, and I serve as executive director of one of the contract operations of the Atomic Energy Commission. . . . I am clearly speaking as a fellow prisoner and sinner and, moreover, as one whose share in the corporate apostasy of our age is greater than that of most. ("The Relation of the Christian College to the Scientific World," in *The Christian Scholar*, Autumn, 1954, p. 253. Used by permission.)

These words are subject to misunderstanding unless read from the perspective afforded by faith. The individual ultimately committed to the validity of the scientific search for knowledge will react against them because they seem to qualify the object of his total trust. No man with a perspective such as Pollard's could seem able to give his "heart and soul" to the scientific enterprise understood as a goal in itself. Pollard would certainly not keep his job if he had expressed such qualifications about it in the Soviet Union. The idealistic moralist in our culture might argue that Pollard should resign a job about which he has such reservations and find a job to which he can devote himself unreservedly. However, if there was a job to which Pollard could devote himself in such a manner, it would then become a source of idolatry.

It is precisely because Pollard perceives and acknowledges the spiritual dangers in the vocation in which he is engaged that it becomes the channel by which his relationship to God is deepened and enriched. He keeps the job, yet transcends it too. It is set into the context of stewardship by a theological understanding that realizes the dangers of its becoming an object of total surrender. A frank admission of the potential misuse guards its valid use. It takes candor to write as Pollard does—a candor born of humble dependence upon the grace of a God who enables men to acknowledge the temptations open to them. Such candor is usual only when the person who has it feels especially secure as an individual.

The element of physical risk has always been an aspect of exploration and conquest. One must risk his safety to learn more about distant lands, ocean depths, cosmic heights. Fortunately, the human spirit is capable of the heroism that will risk life in order to increase human knowledge of unknown spheres. But there is a spiritual risk in such an enterprise—a risk more subtle to perceive and more difficult to understand. This spiritual risk is composed in part of the moral dimension, as with the possible misuse of nuclear power for the total destruction of human life, but even more it involves the possibility that the conquest of nature will become an object of ultimate concern, usurping the place of the Creator himself. Only when men undertake science as a form of stewardship can they offset the dangers of such a temptation and find in their science a channel that enhances their relationship to God rather than substitutes for it.

It is coercive struggle that produces the greatest effort to destroy the other—open, blatant, and often frightening efforts at the liquidation of a foe. Can the security of the justified self ameliorate the fury of coercive struggle? Upon the answer to this query hangs both the extent and the quality of the contribution that religious faith can make toward the solution of one of the most pressing problems of our day—total war.

All theories of the just war are rooted to a large extent in a set of moral considerations presupposing that the participant who claims his cause is just has examined his motives and actions under the scrutiny of external standards. The results of such a scrutiny may be better in theory than in performance, but the possibility remains that appeal to the criteria of the just war implies the willingness of the self to submit its case to the arbitration of moral considerations. The just war evaporated when the nations ceased to acknowledge any possibility of judgment over their actions and thus became laws unto themselves.

To be sure, that group or nation undertaking a military enterprise based upon moral considerations does not lay down its arms and run with haste to embrace an invading army. But neither does it transform the legitimate intention of repelling an invader into an excuse for completely annihilating him! The enemy is considered an enemy only in terms of the substantive threats to justice and order implicit in his overt acts of aggression; he is not transformed into the devil himself whose utter destruction is considered the prime objective.

The term "unconditional surrender" is incompatible with a valid theory of a just war. It may have merits, though dubious ones at that, in creating frenzied zeal in battle, but its military disadvantages outweigh its values and its spiritual corrosions are incalculably bad. An enemy will not hasten to surrender under terms that involve total submission to another nation's will and may even prefer furious and suicidal resistance to total subjugation. Spiritually, the nation that demands total surrender as the price of peace is seeking to seize absolute control in the political realm.

It takes a genuine security of the self to state war aims in specific and well-defined terms, to demand only limited victories for defined objectives, and to exercise responsible self-constraint in the pursuit of such objectives. At least this much is presupposed by George F. Kennan, writing of war and diplomacy in our day, and of what would be necessary to preserve a future war from doing more harm than good.

The first part of this task is a negative one: not to let ourselves be diverted by irrelevant or confusing concepts of war aims. We can avoid, this time, the tyranny of slogans. We can avoid confusing ourselves with grandiose and unrealistic, or even meaningless, phrases designed simply to make us feel better about the bloody and terrible business in which we are engaged. We can remember that war—a matter of destruction, brutalization and sacrifice, of separations, domestic disintegration, and the weakening of the deeper fabrics of society—is a process which of itself can achieve no positive aims: that even military victory is only the prerequisite for some further and more positive achievement which it makes possible but by no means assures. We can have the moral courage, this time, to remind ourselves that major international violence is, in terms of the values of our civilization, a form of bankruptcy for us all—even for those who are confident they are right. (*American Diplomacy: 1900–1950*, pp. 137 f. This material originally appeared in *Foreign Affairs*, published by the Council on Foreign Relations.)

The attitude of Abraham Lincoln during the war that rent our nation asunder constitutes one of the most illustrious demonstrations of the intended amelioration of social struggle in the annals of Western culture. To be sure, Lincoln was less successful in persuading his associates to practice his compassionate sense of justice than he was in phrasing it in memorable words that held "malice toward none." Lincoln fought the war with confidence in the justice of his cause and with resolution to reunite the nation—yet he understood the enterprise as a tragedy rather than as a crusade and he made no pretentious claims for the righteousness of his own endeavor. It is clear that Lincoln gained his poise from a profound though unconventional understanding of religious faith—an understanding that made explicit allowance for the limitations of virtue on his own side as well as in his opponents. Thus he referred to the people as the "almost chosen" and was troubled as much by the fury in the North as by the resistance in the South. John C. Bennett has succinctly caught the picture:

Lincoln exemplified, as hardly any other political leader has done, the commitment to the cause he was called upon to defend without identifying that cause with the will of God in absolute terms. He was strong and resolute without self-righteousness. He saw his cause and the opposing cause under the judgment of God, whose will could not be identified with either one. He could thus respect the integrity of the foe and prepare for dealing mercifully with him in his defeat. (*Christianity and Crisis,* February 8, 1960, pp. 2 f.)

Many commentators on Christian morality during the past two or three decades have drawn sharp distinctions between the kind of concern for others that should mark personal morality and the harsh justice required in official acts of power morality. According to this point of view one can afford kindness and charity in relationships that are face-to-face, but the statesman must do his duty as the responsible instrument of the system he is destined to preserve. A judge may smile at the prisoner in the corridor but he must sentence him in the courtroom; a general may admire the skill of his opponent but must nevertheless seek his annihilation on the field of battle. Butterfield has challenged this point of view on the grounds that humility is as possible in the larger relationships as it is in the smaller ones:

I do not see why in politics even the virtues that I associate with the Christian religion should be suspended for a moment. I mean humility, charity, self-criticism, and acceptance of the problem that Providence sets before one; also a disposition not to seek or direct affairs as though one had a right to assert a sovereign will in the world—a disposition rather to see that one's action takes the form of co-operation with Providence. (*International Conflict in the Twentieth Century*, p. 16.)

Butterfield is able to overcome the dichotomy between personal and political morality because he defines Christian virtue in terms of humility before God rather than in terms of an attained human ideal. He does not suggest that Christian virtue is a sentimental kind of sweetness that ignores responsibility for justice and order, but a unique way of seeking such ends. Christian virtue is a lack of pretension to absolute goodness. The secure self will know its foibles and limitations, admit them, and not seek the destruction of another self in order to bolster its own sense of importance.

We must learn to conduct struggle without the wild demand for absolute victory of our cause. The sloganizing that Kennan decries is a form of idolatry and not merely a case of political bad judgment; it will be cured only by a fully religious corrective and not merely a little wiser political judgment. To be sure, conventional and institutional religion may not have much to contribute, since such forms of religion only mirror the false allegiance of the culture rather than form a basis of judgment over it. But it is both possible and necessary that we do better.

Everett Knight has remarked that our present task is "to revive political enthusiasm without the fanaticism" (*The Objective Society*, p. 10). He goes on to warn us against two religious types—the messiah and the monk. The messiah believes so completely in his cause that he sees all life in terms of his own crusade and bends everything else to bring his cause to fruition. The monk falls asleep to the realities of the political life and withdraws. Both the messiah and the monk would lead us astray: "Between these two we can come to no good" (*ibid.*).

Neither the messiah nor the monk believes in the justi-

fication of the self. Neither sees the self as fully involved
in those contradictions and uncertainties that make both
self-righteousness and escape impossible for man. The one
absolutizes struggle; the other shuns it. We plead for its
amelioration. If we are to become mature, we must avoid
both fanaticisms and lethargies. We must learn the art of
conducting long, slow, steady campaigns against all
dangers rather than hasty and unbridled crusades against
a temporary scapegoat. The pride, self-righteousness, and
fanatical devotion that have sustained morale in times of
war will not suffice for conducting a cold war or undertaking the slow, frustrating drudgery of disarmament negotiations and "police" action in spots of tension and potential trouble. The kind of heroism called for by the war
of words in the United Nations will tax the spiritual
patience of a people that has heretofore shown its capacity
for heroism and devotion only in response to the enthusiasms and slogans of hot wars.

A people accustomed to bouncing enthusiasms and
exuberant response to successes will find its greatest moral
tests to result from the lack of any neat, clear way by
which the problems it faces can be significantly resolved.
There is urgent need for a basis of security that can keep a
nation from great anxiety as it faces perilous and difficult
times. Unfortunately, much of our religious outlook, like
much of our cultural temper, is not geared to appropriate
this sort of maturity. Our involvements with struggle in
its absolutized and idolatrous forms has been long engendered and is still reinforced by the culture that surrounds us. The pattern is not to be broken overnight, even
by "conversions." We sometimes see better that alleys are
blind-ended when we are caught in them than when we are
speeding unmolested down the highways of success. We
still get a thrill out of some radical public protest against
a missile base or rocket launching (if committed to disarmament) or out of the development of a new weapon

(if committed to the arms race) but the lifelong task of mastering technical information and personal maturity in order to become a successful negotiator in disarmament conferences is less exciting. Unless we can make religious sense out of the latter instead of the former we are not likely to make it through the next decades.

Negotiation in disputes is frequently better carried out by hardheaded professionals—each admittedly representing the self-interest of his client but personally rather detached from the controversy—than it is by men dedicated to idealistic causes or sworn to preserve some cultural value. Labor negotiators are best qualified when they are able to assess factors of power and production and the realities of the market, not when they have abstract ideals about distributive justice. Generals may negotiate better during wartime than politicians whose prestige is at stake in the outcome of negotiations. Career diplomats who work behind the scenes can do better at times in international relations than public figures debating in full view from the floor of the General Assembly of the United Nations. A "deal" made by subtle negotiations between nations may do more to ease a situation than strongly announced statements of intended policy from which it is difficult to back down without the loss of face.

We are speaking of the amelioration of struggle, not its elimination. Men must continue their participation in political life but they ought to bring a new contribution to such participation, a contribution that may be derived in some measure from sober religious faith. We have heard a great deal about the need to negotiate from positions of strength, but we have conceived of such strength too much in purely military terms. We need to hear more about the need to negotiate from positions of secure flexibility. The flexibility may be hardheaded but it must spring from a kind of spiritual security that is just as important to genuine experimentation with new procedures in the field of disarmament as from a bargaining position maintained by stockpiles of weapons. Accepted patterns of national self-interest are too rigid to allow a greater self-interest to be served by devising systems of controlled and inspected disarmament, even though idealistically inspired admonitions to unilateral disarmament may be too sentimental to be relevant. We may also need to face the fact that even with the best will in the world we cannot be sure of succeeding in setting up satisfactory possibilities in this area. Our prime task is to be sure that we are not the major obstacle to progress.

There are religions that suggest the self should find its ultimate security in "another world," but this must not preclude the proper concern for how the self relates itself to the issues of the present. The Christian man does not cease to struggle because he knows God's love in his life, but he ceases to regard his personal security as bound entirely to the outcome of the immediate battle. Without ceasing to care what happens in struggle he ceases to care wholly for what happens to his own self or its status. In the extreme situation even martyrdom can be accepted— not in a final thrust to make a public show of loyalty or as an ingenious way of winning the battle—but from full fidelity to the truth to which one is committed. Even death may be given meaning in the context of loyalty to God whereas in life without such a relationship it can only mean defeat.

Because a true relationship to God furnishes the self with a valid security, the self can in turn embrace the neighbor rather than seek his destruction. Conquest is turned to stewardship; competition is purged of its bitter rancor; coercion is reserved for the attainment of specific and well-defined justice.

VIII

MORAL ARROGANCE AND POLITICAL WISDOM: THE TRANSFORMATION OF SOCIAL CHANGE

TENSION and conflict between the defenders of an existing order and those seeking to change it seem perennial. Some decades ago the headlines were filled with reports of violence surrounding the attempts of labor to organize giant industries; today they are filled with reports of violence visited upon those seeking to break down legal walls that segregate men of different colors in a land that professes the equality of all. These tensions between the defender and the revolutionary can be very taut, and the relationship can be marked by bitter antagonism. The spiritual cohesiveness of a human community can be rent asunder by the tensions that result from resistance offered to attempted social change. At times the price extracted seems almost to cancel the results achieved, and the community remains as divided after reform as before the effort was initiated to undo injustice. Can men learn to sublimate the processes by which social changes are made and to meliorate the consequences for those who are called upon to pay high personal prices for new public gains?

The attitudes men bring to social struggle greatly affect, not only the sides they take within it, but the way they conduct themselves on their chosen side. This con-

126

duct in turn affects the consequences that flow from their advocacy and action on behalf of a chosen cause. Their attitudes may be as crucial for the outcome of a movement or campaign as the confessed aims of their partisanship. The manner in which a cause is embraced is as important as the cause to which commitment is made. It is as dangerous to espouse the right end in the wrong way as it is to espouse a wrong end. The consequences that flow from subversion of good motives are sometimes as devastating as the deliberate service of malicious ends. Good causes can be harmed as much by the behavior of their advocates as they are stifled by the opposition of their enemies.

The following discussion contrasts two modes of behavior in social conflict. The one may be called brittle, the other flexible. The one girds its loins for moral battle and erects defenses against all interchange with its antagonists; the other accepts the tensions and jockeyings of social struggle as the given nature of political activity and the only avenue to effective social growth. The one would defend or effect an absolute right; the other would detour around an intolerable wrong. The one crusades; the other negotiates. These two modes of behavior are theoretically in contrast and practically in tension. The difference between them cuts across the normal partisanships on social issues, for liberal programs may be espoused with brittle arrogance and conservative policies may be advocated with poise and flexibility, even though in many instances the reverse seems to be the case.

The determined, zealous, and protective posture of many participants in social struggle must be set in contrast to a candid and melioristic one. The contrast between these two postures may be a greater contrast than the contrast between liberal and conservative policy positions. It is possible to be a brittle conservative or a brittle liberal, to shun the company and shut the door against all who do not agree with one's point of view regardless of the point of view one holds. Intolerance and arrogance appear in crusading liberals as well as in defending conservatives. The revolutionary may be even more willing than the defender of the *status quo* to consign enemies to firing squads. If the intolerances of the Inquisition give witness to the capacity of entrenched powers to commit atrocities in defense of established order, atrocities in modern revolutionary movements give witness to the capacity of challengers to commit atrocities in the effort to hasten social change.

Men's attitudes toward social institutions may reflect this same contrast. How, for instance, shall we look upon the character and function of the United Nations? Here is an organization that stands at the vortex of social change and is designed to ameliorate the agonies of social conflict. Some men describe it as an association of peace-loving peoples (with an embarrassing exception perhaps). They think of this world organization as the protector of justice and order in the world. Deeply committed to this ideal, such individuals would limit membership in the organization to those nations which demonstrate adherence to the principles of justice and order that international life should take on. Qualification for membership is understood less as a function of national power and position than it is seen as a function of moral intention and purpose. Membership is for the morally qualified, not for potentially troublesome members of the family of nations. Other men describe the United Nations as a debating platform—as a place where nations can vent their frustrations with oratory rather than compound them for the battlefield. According to this view the organization is less an association of peace-loving peoples than it is a gathering ground for individual states seeking their own interests, less a protected club of the morally qualified than an arena for verbal contests and diplomatic haggling.

Several kinds of neonationalists distrust the agonized

haggles in the United Nations, because they frustrate the will of the home nation. "Why associate," these people ask, "with a group that lets so many different and often malicious nations have the same voice and the same vote as more civilized nations?" Withdrawal is set forth as the necessary means to preserve moral integrity as well as national independence. We should "go it alone." These demands for nationalistic independence spring less from gross selfishness than from a moral rigidity that cannot see itself involved in any group composed of nations whose purposes are at variance with what is understood to be honorable and decent in world affairs. If the United States withdraws from the United Nations because another communistic country gains admission, the withdrawal will be prompted by this sort of outlook. Moral purity rather than political expediency will be the rationale behind the move.

Idealistic forms of internationalism may be no less disenchanted with the United Nations and its agonized frustrations than neo-isolationist nationalism seems to be. Rather than to suggest withdrawal, the idealists are apt to demand that the United Nations be made stronger by subordinating all national sovereignties to its dominion. Even if such a transformation could be effected, the question surely begs itself as to whether the realities of the present situation would significantly change. After all, is the United States Congress a gathering of moral idealists creating structures of virtue or an arena for verbal contests between conflicting interests and party haggling between power factions?

Those who look upon the legislative process as the operation of virtue for the preservation of order and the extension of good have a very different conception of their role in that process than do those who look upon the legislative process as a conflict and juggling of influence. We can leave to social scientists the elaboration of this distinction, which is basic for the theory and art of government. Our task is to observe that behind these two views of government may lie an even more basic disagreement concerning morality in relationship to struggle. Theological differences and spiritual attitudes are bound into these contrasts as surely as water is bound into the molecule of sugar.

Perhaps we should listen to the preaching of those who exhort us to stand up for what we think is right. Perhaps we should give ear to the arguments that suggest the present plight of the world to be compounded of compromise engaged in by those without the conviction to enforce their ideals upon a recalcitrant and unruly social order. Perhaps a clear declaration of our convictions and a firm resolve to implement them would do much to clear the air, to dispel the fog that engulfs our deliberations, and to insure that social change is piloted to morally righteous ends. Perhaps we can meet the challenge of communism only by having a zeal as high and a moral certainty as complete as is their devotion to the Marxist cause. Perhaps only by inflexible stands, clearly announced in advance to the enemies of freedom, together with ultimatums saying, "Thus far and no farther; so much and no more," can we be faithful to our charge as defenders of righteousness and truth. Perhaps the day of diplomatic flexibility should be over, if indeed it ought ever to have begun, and principle should take precedence over strategy, and righteousness be held dearer than success. Perhaps we should recapture a clear conviction of the right and spurn organizations that cannot effect it or that let in members who give credence to another set of values. Perhaps we should decide that negotiation in human affairs is a futile business and that the attempt to work out solutions tolerable to as many people as possible is merely the road to the satisfaction of none.

The crusader and the moralist would urge us along such

a line. They appeal for the uncompromising allegiance of dedicated men—men willing to struggle for their view of the right and to sacrifice for the preservation of their ideals. Just as a tool best keeps a cutting edge when made of brittle metal, this view of social responsibility relies upon the brittleness of stern conviction and the hardness of unbending rigor in the pursuit of goals. From such an outlook spring the suggestions of the Moral Re-Armament movement. It argues rigorously for a renewed moral dedication coupled with steadfast refusal to relate ourselves in any but a hostile way to our Communist foes. It argues that zealous conviction can do much to put opponents in flight. "The greatest fear of the Communists, therefore, is that their ideology will be countered by a superior moral ideology. Moral Re-Armament provides the security of an incorruptible leadership." (*Ideology and Co-existence,* p. 21.)

The new type of man that Moral Re-Armament is producing finds that the basic problem of industry is not economic but moral. The four moral standards—absolute honesty, absolute purity, absolute unselfishness, absolute love—make it possible to decide issues on the basis of *what is right* and not *who is right*. (*Ibid.,* p. 13.)

But the psychology of protective exclusiveness that marks the moralistic crusader may betray even his professed ideals by the rigid exclusiveness of his position. How indeed can we speak of "absolute love," yet propose to deal with human life in terms of an uncompromising separation of ourselves from those who will not accept our standards? Jesus took issue with the Pharisees for their exclusive withdrawal, for their hostility toward publicans and sinners. By their exclusiveness the Pharisees created division in the name of purity. How can we decide our policies on the basis of what is right rather than who is right except as we are prepared for unsavory bedfellows

from time to time? Those who condemn any social program merely because the Communists might support it
actually invite the enemy to give a kiss of death to any
cause it wishes to destroy. If we cannot decide what is
wrong by observing who espouses a cause, neither can we
decide what is right by looking at who opposes it. Independence, yes; exclusiveness, no.

The fundamental spiritual battle is against brittle self-
righteousness, which visits fury upon those with whom it
disagrees. Moral pretension is a genuine enemy of authentic selfhood as well as grit in the machinery of social
change. It has no place in a proper understanding of
Christian love as an ethical style. We have cited the example of Christ, who took issue with the Pharisees and
became a neighbor to sinners. But other lines of thought
lead to the same conclusion. If, for example, Christian
love is not a moral code but an impulse to become a
Christ to our neighbors in all those situations in which
we find our fellowmen, then it is a thrust toward compassion and candor—away from crusading arrogance. If
Christian love means anything, it means that we need not
be legalists in order to be virtuous or zealots in order to
be good. It may even mean that we are least virtuous when
we are self-righteously concerned about our goodness.
Moral pretension is a genuine threat to neighborliness.

Candor and flexibility are not to be confused with
namby-pamby sentimentality. The first is secure and determined, the second soft and unable to serve any ends.
The first may be expressed in group customs and the conduct of human affairs, the second in largely a personal
attitude. The first may be rigorously defended as a way of
life worthy of allegiance and cultivation; the second lacks
the vigor of conviction and is not structured into the social
life of man. The first is rooted in that security of the self
attained from the justifying gift of grace; the second is
trying earnestly to prove its own goodness by means of

soft virtues substituted for hard ones. The first embodies merely the harmlessness of doves; the second couples to it the wisdom of a properly dedicated serpent.

A sense of wholesome flexibility can be gained from study of the prophetic temperament. In some ways the prophets were rigid and inflexible in their allegiance to the right but in addition they exercised rigorous self-scrutiny that held even the righteous nation up to the judgment of God. The moral absolutism of the prophets is different from the moral absolutism of the crusader. In the case of the crusader the interests and behavior of his own group are made absolute, and the forces of evil and darkness are all pictured in control of the other side. In the case of the prophet the interests and behavior of his own group are called into question before a transcendent conception of holiness that effectively judges the short-comings in both parties to a social conflict. If the crusader is tempted to the indiscriminate identification of his cause with the ultimate good, the prophet may be tempted to erase the discriminate judgments that are necessary between relative social values, but the latter error is less dangerous than the former.

By bringing the home nation to judgment and humility the prophet may prevent the self-righteousness that so easily accompanies dedication to some moral cause. The prophetic temper stands as a safeguard against turning relatively important causes into objects of idolatrous loyalty. Prophetic absolutism is an effective alternative to the absolutism of the crusader precisely because it roots its final trust in the ultimate God rather than in some earthly cause, however valuable that cause may be.

If the behavior of men in conflict situations is to be responsible and well-bounded, something of the prophetic temper must be at work. If nations are to conduct just wars for legitimate moral objectives, the prophetic sense of the overarching righteousness by which all men are judged must be so vivid that the nation cannot be carried away by the passions of conflict and the thirst for victory into those excessive zeals that result in absolutized war. It is not enough to recognize with the political analysts that wars for undefined objectives are dangerous or with the military analysts that slogans like "unconditional surrender" are stupid. We must also find the spiritual resources by which we add to political and military judgments the spiritual candor to effect the changes in our own procedures that such insights require.

The prophetic scrutiny of human life can also serve to ferret out sores in the social order before they erupt into open conflict. Alertness to the need for change, watchfulness against corruption and injustice, warnings against lethargies and false allegiances may all appear as contributions of the prophet to the transformation of social change. The prophet does not align himself uncritically with the *status quo* any more than he becomes a self-righteous crusader. Moreover, the prophet may heighten our sense of proportion by pointing out what is essential and what is accidental in a social system. Many changes are possible in human life without altering the fundamental loyalty of men. Great struggles sometimes develop between defenders and their adversaries when the adversaries seek to change one of the accidental arrangements that legitimately could go. We ought to know what must be kept and what is expendable in order that flexibility about indifferent affairs remains a genuine possibility. The truest liberal is less the person with a program to advocate than he is the person who scrutinizes every existing social arrangement with the wisdom to know what should be kept and what should be changed and the willingness to go about the process within the structures of accepted procedure. The central allegiance of the liberal is to those structures of accepted procedure that make orderly change possible short of coercion and violence.

Philosophies of political realism that teach us about the use of power and influence within the dynamics of social action must not push off the stage those crucial insights of more idealistic thinking that focus on the means by which such power and influence are bent into constructive and positive ends and channeled to the proper purposes. Christian ethical thought has no vocation to identify itself completely with a cynical theory of *Realpolitik* even though by its understandings of human sinfulness it is guarded against overly bland hopes and optimistic idealisms. A balance of power conception of government is not merely a device for exercising power or checking tyranny any more than it is a device for translating high idealism into political reality. It is a shrewd device, informed by a just balance of suspicion and hope, for insuring orderly procedure in the conduct of government. It is a device to which we should give positive allegiance and meaning even when its operation seems clumsy and ill-fated. There is no mandate in the Christian doctrine of sin that allows us to become advocates of the free and open brawl even though we are not permitted the luxury of illusions about the smooth and idyllic operation of the body politic.

The flexibility of which we speak may also be epitomized in the conception of "his majesty's loyal opposition." Such an opposition is dependent for its existence upon two crucial factors. On the one hand, the majority must tolerate the right of the minority to disagree—openly and frankly. On the other hand, the minority must exercise this right with responsibility and in obedience to the existing laws of the social order. Neither condition is fostered in absolutized struggle—for a majority totally convinced of its righteous exercise of power would regard the toleration of a minority as a dilution of its own devotion to the truth, while a minority bent on the destruction rather than the helpful criticism of the majority would destroy the social balance.

We find many illustrations of an intolerant majority. Some of these come from religiously engendered feelings that error does not deserve the privileges accorded to the truth, and result in inquisitions; others involve political regimes in which the liquidation of opposition is treated as the right of the ruling party, and result in totalitarian atrocities. The toleration of loyal opposition is an essential ingredient in a healthy democratic government. Deliberate attention must be paid to the preservation of the minority's rights to be heard, to have its redress in court, to criticize the policies of the dominant groups, and to seek to win sufficient backing for its point of view to become in turn the new majority. This seems so elemental that its repetition runs the danger of being platitudinous —but the spiritual condition in which this sort of process can occur is a tender flower that needs the constant watering of rehearsed defense.

To be sure, a prime requirement is loyalty in the opposition. In a day when two giant systems of political life are locked in crucial conflict and the agents of one are infiltrated throughout the other it is difficult to distinguish between loyal opposition and dangerous subversion. There are those who would rather err on the side of safety and infringe the rights of minorities than to leave the nation exposed to the dangers of a disloyal minority. But carried to its logical limits this position is itself subversive, for by curtailing the right of opposition—more by frenzied types of public intolerance than by structured inquisitions or political liquidations—this approach would divest the democratic culture of that very inner criticism most essential to its health.

Toleration of a loyal opposition is temperamentally difficult for the crusading moral absolutist. The more completely he becomes devoted to the defense of his own position the less he will be tolerant of divergent points of view. When so much religion seems to support self-righteousness, profounder forms of faith must come forward with protests and warnings. These protests can be lodged against all forms of fanatical devotion, religious or secular as the case may be.

Politicians at work are bound to give the moral sense a bit of a shock. In the national nominating convention of 1960, John Kennedy and Lyndon Johnson were found on the opening days making sharp and bitter charges of each other's unfitness for nomination to the presidential office. But later in the week, when one of them had won first place on the ticket and had invited the other as a running mate, Lyndon Johnson remarked that he had always been a friend of Jack Kennedy. Such a change of relationship might suggest that politicians are two-faced, that they don't really believe what they say, and that they will swallow any contradiction when it is to their advantage to do so. But consider the results of a contrary course of action. Suppose the politicians insisted that all they had said in times of opposition was so completely right that healing of breaches and mending of fences was impossible. Suppose they applied slogans such as "total victory" and "unconditional surrender" to the political process. Only division could come from such absolutism. The possibility of democratic decision-making within a convention would be altogether destroyed by a situation in which opposition could dare to show its face only in the knowledge that if it failed to carry an issue, it would be banished from the group. Political conventions may be the despair of moralists, but we may render daily thanks that moralists don't conduct the affairs of party politics.

The healing process described with respect to the political convention is possible because loyalty to party is stronger in each side of the disagreement than allegiance to its own position. Likewise, when two political parties enter the public contest in November we fall behind the winning side because loyalty to the nation is stronger than loyalty to the partisan group. Perhaps this is to say that the effective possibilities of his majesty's loyal opposition depend in the final sense upon the presence of his majesty. "His majesty" is a symbol or reality commanding stronger loyalties than any of the lesser causes to which men are drawn. If there is no standard or person to which all men can repair, then indeed what are we to do?

The international conflicts of the twentieth century seem to be conflicts over which there is no majesty. There seems to be no standard to which both sides in conflict can repair, and the struggle becomes the brutal and bitter effort to survive. When in Sunday school we heard that the brotherhood of man was possible only under the Fatherhood of God we were intrigued by the logic and excited by the vision. As we grew older the whole dream seemed so utopian that its sentimentality overshadowed the logic, and we could only make meaning of the conflict in terms of the balance of power. But the original vision is worth reiteration if only as a witness to the fact that— eschatologically, if you like—the great conflicts of our age will be transformed only if and when the ultimate majesty that stands above all men is given due affirmation. There may be no transformation of social change short of this implied unity of final loyalty. Even under such a loyalty, however, conflict would continue in a different form. We might even see the United Nations resemble a political convention and deem it a great improvement.

Meanwhile our vocation is to act in response to the ideals we understand and not to ape those who turn conflict into rancor by the unmitigated pursuit of their own purposes. We must maintain our allegiance to those processes and attitudes in which we find profound meaning and in which we place our eventual confidence. In addition to prophetic self-scrutiny and toleration of a loyal opposition we need to cultivate integrity in debate and compassion in reform.

The political process will always involve verbal exchanges and heated arguments between parties that see a problem from different perspectives. Protagonist and antagonist will always need to battle issues with their wits. But the art of democratic controversy is a subtle business and is easily perverted from its noble function. Every student of college logic can recognize an *ad hominem* argument when illustrated on a philosophy quiz but when he encounters such an argument in campus politics or outside life his scent is not so keen. And when in later years he finds such arguments useful for his purposes he may even forget he ever learned to detect them.

Is it too little to ask that integrity mark the oratory and debate that surrounds the conflicts of our day? If the attempt to destroy the other involves the use of the smear and the jeer which downgrade him as a person instead of attacking the issue for which he stands, are not Christians enjoined to scruples about the arguments they utter? Integrity in debate requires studied knowledge of the issues, cogent analysis of the problems, and scrupulous refusal to resort to smear tactics in order to gain victory.

Perhaps an even greater burden for demanding integrity in debate rests with those who listen than with those who orate. As long as juries seemingly are swayed by the impassioned oratory of lawyers the temptation for the bar to employ phrases with emotional appeal is well-nigh irresistible. As long as politicians gain public acclaim and attention by the use of smear techniques we are bound to see the continuation of campaigns that gain their ends by employing such tactics. The witch-hunt will go away when people no longer believe in witchcraft. Political smear techniques will go away when people learn to demand solid and substantial advocacy of policy matters in the campaign oratory to which they are exposed. We can do our bit to hasten this day, but we should be warned against expecting it to arrive at an early date. Meanwhile we may exercise the prophetic function of calling to public attention all forms of political life that fall short of the integrity they ought to possess.

Moreover, we are called to have compassion in reform. All social changes involve disruptions for certain groups. At times it seems that these groups get what is coming to them and that just retribution grinds out the sentences with unflinching regularity. Oppressors are overthrown—then spit upon. The privileged are cast down—and trampled underfoot. Those who wield great power become in turn the outcasts—and live as haunted men. The defender holds to his power beyond its just exercise, and when the adversary strikes him down he does so with vengeance and in wrath.

The revolutionary temper is impatient with the groups it overthrows and by taking vengeance upon those formerly in power becomes in turn a new source of tyranny. We have lived in a period when the liquidation of former enemies is standard operating procedure in many political systems. The instability born of revolutionary change is compounded with the bitterness that attends a shift in power. The fury of communism is illustrative of the attempt to destroy the enemies of revolution. Such a destruction is carried out from idealistic rather than from cynical motives—for the committed Marxist truly believes that when the enemies of the system have been eliminated the temporary tyranny of the revolutionary period will come to a permanent end.

If the revolutionary may be compared with a hatchet man, the Christian may be compared with the surgeon. The surgeon may need to cut in order to heal, and the use of the scalpel is not without pain. But the surgeon cuts with compassion, whereas the hatchet man chops with fury. The surgeon cuts with controlled touch and with careful calculation; the hatchet man swings wildly at all that seems to get in his way. The surgeon salves and sews up the wound; the hatchet man lets the flesh lie raw. The Christian use of power must be a controlled and compassionate use of necessary means to morally legitimate ends. It must not give way to the frenzy of the fanatic.

Compassion in reform may well embrace the truly crucial implications in Jesus' teaching about love for enemies. In his teaching, Jesus laid upon his followers a duty to be fair and just in the treatment of those with whom they came in conflict. Love for enemies has frequently been interpreted as an injunction to avoid conflict itself, but may it not have significance for behavior within conflict? As an injunction to compassion in reform it would hold out a viable and cogent alternative to the realities of a time in which reform is so frequently attended by vindictiveness and the fight for a cause made into the excuse to destroy all that stands in the way of its attainment.

At the close of the Second World War an editorial appeared in *Christianity and Crisis* illustrating the kind of Christian attitude that can transform conflict—not by altering its external conditions but by remaking the attitudes men hold about it. It is not only a proof that such an attitude is possible but when compared with some editorial comment at the time becomes an indication of how far many are from attaining to it:

However we measure the conflict, whether in terms of the evil we opposed, or the evils we had to commit in opposing it, or the destruction of the vanquished or the price of the victors, the dimensions of the drama in which we are involved are staggering. It is well that we should be shocked into sobriety by the magnitude of historical events and should be prompted to humility and piety by a contemplation of the tasks which still confront us. All of them are really beyond our best wisdom.

They [occupation, preventing starvation] will not be done too well in any event because of their magnitude; but they will be done with a greater degree of wisdom if they are done with a measure of humility. If we had more awe before the tragic punishments which God has already visited upon a nation which took law into its own hands, we would at least be saved the folly of spoiling the divine punishment by our own efforts to add or subtract. We might well remember that the greatest difficulty which a vanquished nation finds in turning from the "sorrow of this world" (despair) to the "sorrow of God" (repentance) is that the pride of the victor tends to obscure the divine punishments.

Let us therefore not seek to reduce the dimension of the history in which we are involved, so that it might be made more compatible with the limits of our powers. Let us recognize that we have faced the mystery of evil and of good, of tragedy and of victory, of divine punishment and mercy in more tremendous proportions than ever before in history. The humble consciousness of the inadequacy of our wisdom for the tasks which confront us may infuse our wisdom with grace and thus render it more adequate for the issues that we must face. (May 28, 1945, pp. 1 f.)

An increase of this spirit would not in itself eliminate all traces of discord or tension from the processes of social change, but it would go far to make the process more tolerable and its consequences less precarious. Surely the Christian cannot refuse to work for the small gains that would be wrought by this spirit shed abroad more widely in the lives of men.

IX

A SOUND BASIS FOR ZEAL: THE SUBLIMATION OF THE CRUSADE

LIFE lived in response to God consists of holding many lesser loyalties in subordination to one ultimate and commanding devotion—not in order that the lesser loyalties be spurned but in order to embrace them in a more sustained and sustaining framework of meaning. The primacy of the ultimate trust as conceived in Biblical faith is consistent with human devotion to lesser causes unless and until such devotion makes the lesser causes into rival absolutes. Man's devotion to God is not diminished by his attempted conquest of nature as long as such conquest is undertaken in recognition of man's final dependence upon the Creator; man's devotion to God is not diminished by his acceptance of political responsibility unless such political responsibility is embraced as a substitute trust for the God who acts providentially in history; even coercive struggle may be a legitimate means of service unless it becomes a source of devotion to an earthly crusade and admits to no judgment or criticism of itself. The doctrines of Creation and of Providence preserve radical monotheism compatible with man's embrace of life in this world, for as H. Richard Niebuhr has observed: "Radical monotheism dethrones all absolutes short of the principle of being itself. At the same time it reverences every relative existent. Its two great mottoes are: 'I am the Lord thy God; thou shalt have no other gods before me' and 'Whatever is, is good.' " (*Radical Monotheism and Western Culture,* p. 37. Harper & Brothers, 1960. Used by permission.)

The pressures and tensions of struggle, on the other hand, threaten to demand the total time, attention, and devotion of the men who are involved in them. The hard work and sacrifice entailed in struggle frequently create the conditions under which the primacy of God is overlooked. Abnormally high allegiance to even a legitimate purpose may end as a transfer of loyalty. Idolatry is less often a fanaticism of falsified loyalty than it is a matter of excessive abandon to some otherwise proper end. The all-impassioned and uncritical abandon to a cause that conjoins idolatry with partisanship seems to be almost a natural consequence of struggle. It occurs by default rather than conscious rebellion, but it is no less a rejection of God's primacy. The fanaticisms of excess are less easy to detect or to overcome than the fanaticisms of perversity, which display a label on their malcontents. But alas, obedience to the one true God requires that these also be judged and spurned.

The true God is the only reality to which ultimate devotion can be made without the danger of idolatry. Moreover, devotion to the true God may become absolute without becoming idolatrous only in prophetic rather than in priestly terms. Devotion in priestly terms results in a religious idolatry in which the channels of devotion are made into absolutes and the paraphernalia of religion are accorded the degree of exaltation legitimately reserved for God himself. Theological formulations may likewise be accorded more loyalty than the reality to which they point. This occurs with sufficient regularity, so that the wrath of God is frequently visited upon his own spokesmen by the secular world of life and thought. What the same secular world does not understand is that within its own life and thought the very kinds of rigidity it criticizes in the religious sphere appear whenever it affirms some value in an unqualified way. Did not Isaiah understand as much when he addressed himself to Assyria as the rod of Yahweh's anger against his own nation and warned that she in turn would be cut down for her arrogant boasting and for her failure to play her role in obedience to the true God? "When the Lord has finished all his work on Mount Zion and on Jerusalem he will punish the arrogant boasting of the king of Assyria and his haughty pride." (Isa. 10:12.)

One of the most pressing needs of our age is to create a spiritual maturity in which devoted allegiance to a just cause is possible without the excessive enthusiasms that so often seem necessary to maintain morale. If the zeal-to-win is created by a self-delusion that borders on idolatry, how can we give up the false allegiance and still not lose? This is one of the most acute and perplexing questions in our time since the idolatrous foundations for zeal to which we have been accustomed have led us to a situation that is politically dangerous as well as theologically unsound. Can spiritual maturity replace fanaticism in the affairs of men?

Theologians are not fond of quoting generals in illustration of their point, but some time ago the commandant of the Marine Corps made a significant speech on the problem of morale. The speech was delivered in a period in which public clamor for troop indoctrination courses against communism was at a fever pitch and certain branches of the service were instilling hatred of communism in the troops by means of strong modes of teaching. Prompted by repeated questioning from reporters as to whether or not the Marine Corps was developing enough hate, General David Shoup replied through a speech with the following observations:

As far as the Marines are concerned, we try to teach them to be good citizens, to be good soldiers, but we don't indoctrinate hate against anybody.

We're professional soldiers. We fight any enemy the President designates. We don't have to develop hate. We don't just keep talking communism, communism, communism.

I don't think that you have to hate to be a good fighter. A professional boxer doesn't hate his opponent, and as a matter of fact, if he does, he doesn't fight as well. . . .

You might build up a hate against one enemy and find yourself fighting another.

Twenty minutes after the fighting stopped in World War II in the Pacific you saw Marines helping to rehabilitate their former enemies, the Japanese, right on the battlefield. (*The New York Times,* October 28, 1961, p. 41.)

As set forth in this address the duty of the Marine in conflict is to serve in obedience to some authority and not to embrace every battle with ideological abandon. The morale of the Marine is sustained by many rituals and icons but, if the word of his commandant is determinative, these are embraced as subordinate paraphernalia and not as objects of final loyalty. Far down the scale of theological sophistication we thus find illustrated the kind of loyalty-transcendence that it is our purpose to examine as a paradigm for the relationship that Christians hold to God.

The loyalty of the whole Marine Corps was placed by its commandant squarely in the service of the President as the Commander in Chief of the nation. This prevents a particular branch of service from becoming a semiprivate judge of virtue, loyal to its self-chosen causes, and allows, in both practice and theory, greater flexibility in the exercise of duty than any ideological indoctrination could ever provide. The task of the Corps in its commandant's eyes was to do its assigned job rather than to save the whole body politic from the forces of darkness and evil.

But the radical ethical monotheist will need to question the point at which the general stopped in his conception of authority. Is the nation-state the ultimate guardian of virtue, and dare the Christian abandon to it the effective determination of all his loyalties? The earliest Christian refusal to take part in military service was based largely

upon an opposition to the soldier's duty of burning in-
cense at the patriotic shrine as a symbol of his unreserved
loyalty to Caesar. Soldiering itself was less an obstacle than
idolatry that went with it, and the moral question less
clear than the theological one.

It is crucial that we keep clear our lines of devotion.
The Christian is ultimately committed to the God who
stands over all nations and causes. Fortunately, the service
of many causes may be undertaken in loyalty to this God,
presupposing only that the object of final trust is properly
identified. The final source of Christian zeal is not the
immediate battle in which he is engaged but the vocation
by virtue of which he is engaged in the battle in the first
place. The root of this vocation cannot be other than in
abandon to the God who stands above all earthly sources of
value, not in order to negate them but in order to preserve
them from becoming the objects of fanatical idolatry.

With this in mind, consider the motivation that ought
to govern man's attempted conquest of nature. The scientific quest may be legitimately undertaken as a service of
human need and in loyalty to the God of creation. Man's
stewardship—his control of nature bequeathed by God—
is a legitimate and fruitful service when undertaken as an
expression of fidelity to God, but when made into an end
in itself can be a source of bitterness. Undertaken as a
human thrust for power, the scientific enterprise may even
prove disconcerting—for every advance in techniques
creates new problems of control and extracts high prices in
readjustment. The era of electronic machines has not
brought utopia to either those who use them or those who
are used by them. The predictions that 1984 will be a
nightmare are at least as plausible as the expectations that
we shall perpetually have "better things for better living
through chemistry."

It is probably too much that we should ask the scientist today to do his work with the sense of immediate divine compulsion that motivated a Johannes Kepler to end

one of his astronomical works with a prayer, both of gratitude for the light of grace through which he believed his
insights born and with humble petition for forgiveness for
any presumptive misuse of the divine handiwork that he
may have committed. It is probably too much to expect
that scientists should regard their work as "thinking God's
thoughts after him." After all, not all theologians would
qualify by such a test. But we certainly can ask that scientists who understand life in Christian terms resist the
illusory expectations that attend much public adoration
of the technological enterprise.

Late in 1961 a national television network presented a
documentary on weather forecasting and control. Among
other scenes was an interview in which the chief forecaster
of a large Eastern city told of the difficulties in writing
weather forecasts to suit the differing and even conflicting
expectations of the public. Show people want the forecast
so worded as to ensure that people will not be tempted to
stay home on unpleasant evenings, whereas the salesmen
for mufflers and galoshes want the public to know that the
weather will demand protection against the elements. The
documentary went on to survey the technological advances
in forecasting the weather and the initial strides man has
taken toward its control. The implied assumption of the
program was that life will be greatly eased for man when
he has learned to control the weather itself—to soften the
destructive effects of tornadoes and to tone down hurri-
canes. The day of humanly controlled weather was pictured as worth all the cost and sacrifice needed to bring it
about. Nobody asked, in the program at least, who will
decide how the weather is to be controlled when and if
the day comes that it can be. The plight of the forecaster
who cannot now please a divided public was allowed to
cast no shadow over the glories of weather manipulation!
Had some philosopher predicted that the day of weather
control would bring bitter rancor to man as well as legiti-

mate benefits he undoubtedly would have been shown an exit. Must we proceed in delusion about the prospects of a new age in order to believe that it is worth attaining?

Television documentaries probably cannot be expected to explore the implications of Christian stewardship— though this particular program gave a full and sufficient coverage of the Farmer's Almanac! Christians, however, should be expected to listen and observe the subtle adoration of scientific discovery that goes on about them with alert and critical eyes for the values to which it gives allegiance. They may then exercise the prophetic criticism of these loyalties and warn that the scientific quest is under judgment when perpetuated as a self-justifying human enterprise demanding a total and unquestioning devotion. Christians need to cherish no illusions about the ambiguity that attends man's conquest of nature—the possible multiplication of conflict that goes with an increase of power and the intensification of destructive consequences that may attend its use. The Christian may undertake the scientific enterprise as a form of stewardship without manufacturing illusions about the glories it shall someday bring to man. And, if the case demands it for a specific situation, he can qualify or withdraw from the enterprise for the sake of other values without giving up his reason for existence. The Christian is concerned about the spirit in which the scientific enterprise is understood, embraced, and carried out. The scientific quest can be continued without the grasp for omnipotence that largely marks its present pursuit, or the illusory hopes that are often used to make it seem worthwhile.

Hope for man is reborn whenever we rediscover our dependence upon the good earth. That hope will be expressed in a reverent concern that what God has provided shall be used to serve nothing less than His good which is the one real good of all things. (Daniel Day Williams, *God's Grace and Man's Hope*, p. 166.)

A crusade to make the world safe for democracy might elicit little enthusiasm in our day. Our generation may be more cautious about grand promises than its parents were —though in the world as a whole the fantastic promises of revolutionary leaders are still heeded, and the utopian expectations of the Marxist dream of a classless society still fire the imaginations of countless victims of its ideology. What, if anything, has the Christian to lay beside such promises—not merely to keep strong his morale but to appeal to the uncommitted in such a way as to prevent their total servitude to political ideologies that are sustained with hoopla and military campaigns that are conducted with fanfare?

If conflicts are to be pursued with moral sensitivity and kept under the scrutiny of moral criticism, they must be undertaken with an attitude of responsibility and supported with self-critical candor. The motivation must be significantly independent of immediate success even though concerned about the outcome of the struggle. Partial success must have meaning, and failure accepted without utter despair. It is the bold claim of Christian faith that loyalty to God combines the elements of concern and transcendence that such a posture demands. Under loyalty to God we can find good reason to support a cause without having to make it an absolute. Philippe Maury has made a distinction between loyalty and loyalism. By "loyalty" he means a tentative and proper concern for political causes; by "loyalism" he means absolute surrender. In light of this distinction, loyalism is appropriate only to God, but loyalty is possible to secondary concerns. Therefore:

In political matters, in relation to the party or the nation, our loyalty will consist precisely in not hiding that as Christians we reject loyalism [toward political causes]; that our participation in party activities, our devotion to our country will always be limited by our loyalism or absolute loyalty to God. In making clear the nature of this limitation on our political involvement we can demonstrate how total is our dependence upon God, and proclaim that Jesus Christ is Lord. (From *Politics and Evangelism*, pp. 90 f. Copyright © 1959 by Doubleday & Company, Inc. Reprinted by permission.)

The main focus for Christian zeal is gratitude for what God has done, through his mighty acts in history, to visit and redeem his people from all that would ultimately destroy them. But this does not make very good advertising copy for political campaigns, and it is the duty of every Christian to translate the ultimate assurances of the gospel into the sustaining hopes that enable each man to live as unto the Lord while he struggles in the pursuit of justice and political freedom. These hopes must be so engendered that they will be sustained despite setbacks but curbed in case of success. Wise indeed are men who pray to God that in times of adversity they may not suppose that God has forgotten them and that in times of prosperity they may not forget him.

The human spirit was built for life within community. It responds to the sustaining support of kindred spirits who share its purposes and identify themselves with its hopes. Solitary confinement is one of the most effective instruments for destroying the drive and initiative of men because it robs them of that companionship for which they were created. Perhaps community is the true and best foundation for morale—a foundation even deeper in its meaning and more necessary in its presence than belief in the cause for which one fights. In an article on morale in the military services Hanson W. Baldwin has pointed out that knowledge of political objectives is not the most crucial factor in maintaining zeal. "The chief motivational requirement," he writes, "in the indoctrination of a fighting man is pride of uniform, pride of unit, pride of corps, pride of self. The old chestnut that 'I belong to the best damn squad in the best damn platoon in the best damn company,' etc., has provided the basic axiom for military greatness from Caesar's legions and Napoleon's Old Guard to the present." (*The New York Times,* January 12, 1962, p. 7.) Each source of pride mentioned by Baldwin is social in character, save one, and Baldwin himself went on to say that "leadership is the key to good fighting men."

The Christian faith involves membership in a community. Christians who have participated in social crusades, such as freedom rides and resistance movements, report that their morale has been sustained by the feeling of community. In a Southern Negro church, surrounded by a mob of frenzied people and a cordon of police, a group of freedom riders breaks into a hymn: "Lead, Kindly Light, Amid th' Encircling Gloom." The hymn creates renewed dedication, not only because it is sung in the company of kindred believers but because it belongs to the community that God has created in human history. The sustenance flows from the past as well as the present. It is rooted in the experience of covenantal relationship with God and of fellowship with his faithful servants. The experience is reserved for those who belong to the circle of faith. Dietrich Bonhoeffer, who spent the prime years of his life in opposition to Hitler, tells in his letters from prison of the strength derived from the use of hymns and from thinking during his incarcerations of the great feast days of the church. After ten years of torment and persecution he was still able to write:

I believe that God both can and will bring good out of evil. For that purpose he needs men who make the best use of everything. I believe God will give us all the power we need to resist in all time of distress. But he never gives it in advance, lest we should rely upon ourselves and not on him alone. (*Prisoner for God,* p. 21. The Macmillan Company, 1954. Used by permission.)

Christians are bold to declare that the sustaining fellowship of suffering is not confined to men alone. God himself has struggled in this vail of human tears and joys, less to assure his followers immunity from struggle than to ensure that they may undertake it with hope and confidence. How can anyone read the Bible without recognizing that its pages are infused with this understanding? The writer of I Peter urges Christians to rejoice, even though "now for a little while you may have to suffer various trials, so that the genuineness of your faith, more precious than gold which though perishable is tested by fire, may redound to praise and glory and honor at the revelation of Jesus Christ (I Peter 1:6). The writer of Hebrews recites the trials and tribulations of the saints and martyrs and then admonishes his readers to run the race set before them with patience and steadfast endurance.

Great boldness is required to believe that God struggles alongside of men. Religions that would preserve their God from defilement by the world consider the assertion a mockery because it contradicts the majesty of the divine nature. Those searching for statements that fit the canons of tight logic and the tests of verifiability will have doubts about the assertion because it cannot be tested apart from surrender and trust. Christians need not apologize for the fact that this insight is finally dependent upon entrance into a circle of faith. Every insight of equivalent status is likewise dependent upon an analogous surrender, including statements often accepted by the critics of religion. Consider, for example, the great enthusiasm that some men have for the prospects of the scientific method or for the eventual triumph of human reason in bringing justice and peace to the world. Advocates of such views hold to their trust in human achievements despite many and recurrent human failures, since every instance of default can be explained away on the grounds that at a given time and in a given instance man has not yet learned to be sufficiently tolerant or scientific. Those who argue that faithful response to God provides a transformation of struggle when men are properly related to God would seem entitled to say that a man's surrender is faulty or inadequate whenever it appears that it does not work. The secular optimist may protest that man's embrace of scientific objectivity has not seemed to improve things because it is not yet complete; the Christian can certainly say the same thing about man's devotion to God.

The justifying love of God furnishes a resource for relieving the anxiety of the self in the tensions of struggle, not by some magical cure but by the slow, deliberate, and experiential encounter with life understood in this perspective and lived in this trust. We have illustrated this with the freedom riders and with a prisoner for God, but theirs is not the only kind of social struggle. In the cause of racial justice there are many others whose concern is unsung and unpublicized. They know little comfort in the quiet duty they have assumed other than the ability to live at peace with their best selves. These are the men whose estrangement from segregationist kinfolk is as painful as their realization of the injustice that an evil system imposes upon the disenfranchised. They are racked by the disparity between their clarified sense of justice and their bonds of attachment to the perpetuators of a system of injustice. As violence flares they wonder if there is any balm in Dixie, yet they will not settle for a false peace. From one side they may be regarded as fence-sitting moderates, and from the other as traitors to their own heritage. They did not ask for the turmoil of the present conflict, but now that the issue is made they will not settle for less than its proper resolution. Unless we are to argue that there is no role for such individuals we must find for them a sustaining source of zeal that does not stem from the enthusiasm of a crusade.

There is a profound sense in which the sensitive person ought to feel the horror of struggle, to hate involvement even as the prophets resisted their call to preach. The per-

son who is too elated by the prospects of a social struggle
is not likely to conduct it with sensitivity or sustained re-
serve. He will either fire his interest with fanaticism or
grow fearful when the going gets tough. But, as the prophets knew, there can be within men a burning fire, a per-
sistent urge, a strange compulsion toward involvement.
Jeremiah came to know the healing power of God even
though he rebelled against the burdens that he bore as a
prophet. The heights and depths between Jeremiah's bitter
questions and profound experience of faith are a better
clue to the nature of religious encounter with God than
the felt calm of an uneventful routine.

We live in an age—as perhaps all men have done—
when there is a deep impatience with the costly consequences of participation in struggle. If only we could end
the agony by some quick and strongly executed action
done in the name of truth and on behalf of justice! But it
is not given to us to have life on these terms any more than
it has been in God's long dealings with mankind. The
situation of perfect righteousness and obedience does not
come. The resurgence of the radical right and the radical
left in American political life following the long and perplexing tensions of the cold war represent opposite sides
of the same phenomenon. The one attributes the difficulties to our failure to pursue aggressive policies for the
once-and-for-all eradication of evil; the other attributes
our difficulties to a pursuit of aggressive policies at all.
During the Korean War, for example, General MacArthur
and the militant pacifists expressed curiously similar dis-
satisfactions with the official policy, but they would have
cured the situation by opposite prescriptions. Underneath
they are strange bedfellows, each sure that a more rigorous
and consistent allegiance to a clear course of action will
erase the ambiguities from history.

Christians perceive in faith that only one action in history has erased ambiguity—and then only in the ultimate sense. They return from the cross to see an empty tomb but then find the Christian movement itself as marred by human foibles as were the groups that crucified Christ. Apart from faith in the ultimacy of God's victory, the temptations to despair and cynicism are irresistible. Claims for the victory wrought by God must not be set forth in terms that ignore the continual need for it to transform and redeem all the historical life of man. With our hearts attentive to the hope that is attached by faith to these mighty acts of God we may bear faithful obedience to the duties in which we have been placed and maintain a zeal that is not bound to the vicissitudes of fortune. Whether or not we win in the struggle becomes secondary to whether or not we remain faithful to the God we serve. Only from the freedom thus given to us to transform the struggle may we even dare to hope that it shall become the channel of a divine accomplishment.